Willa Cather's

My Antonia

Text by

Tim Wenzell

(M.A., Rutger's University)

Department of English

Middlesex County College

Edison, New Jersey

Illustrations by

Zina Parubchenko

Research & Education Association

Visit our website at

www.rea.com

Research & Education Association
61 Ethel Road West
Piscataway, New Jersey 08854
E-mail: info@rea.com

MAXnotes® for
MY ANTONIA

Published 2017

Printed in the United States of America

Library of Congress Control Number 96-67435

ISBN-13: 978-0-87891-034-2
ISBN-10: 0-87891-034-4

L16

What **MAXnotes**® *Will Do for You*

This book is intended to help you absorb the essential contents and features of Willa Cather's *My Antonia* and to help you gain a thorough understanding of the work. Our book has been designed to do this more quickly and effectively than any other study guide.

For best results, this **MAXnotes** book should be used as a companion to the actual novel, not instead of it. The interaction between the two will greatly benefit you.

To help you in your studies, this book presents the most up-to-date interpretations of every section of the novel, followed by questions and fully explained answers that will enable you to analyze the material critically. The questions also will help you to test your understanding of the novel and will prepare you for discussions and exams.

Meaningful illustrations are included to further enhance your understanding and enjoyment of the literary work. The illustrations are designed to place you into the mood and spirit of the work's settings.

This **MAXnotes** book analyzes and summarizes each section as you go along, with discussions of the characters and explanations of the plot. A biography of the author and examination of the work's historical context will help you put this literary piece into the proper framework of what is taking place.

The use of this study guide will save you the hours of preparation time that would ordinarily be required to arrive at a complete grasp of this work of literature. You will be well prepared for classroom discussions, homework, and exams. The guidelines that are included for writing papers and reports on various topics will prepare you for any added work that may be assigned.

The **MAXnotes** will take your grades "to the max."

Larry B. Kling
Chief Editor

Contents

Each chapter includes List of Characters, Summary, Analysis, Study Questions and Answers, and Suggested Essay Topics.

SECTION ONE

Introduction

The Life and Work of Willa Cather

Willa Cather was born in 1873 in rural Virginia. She moved with her family from Virginia to Red Cloud, Nebraska, at age ten. Red Cloud was a small railroad town that had just been founded thirteen years before the Cathers moved there, populated by immigrants from all over Europe. When Cather attended Red Cloud High School, she became enamored with learning the classics. A townswoman, Mrs. Minor, contributed greatly to her love for music, a love that entered many of the characters in her novels. Ms. Cather began to forge friendships with many of the immigrants that had moved to Red Cloud. Her compassion for their struggles again reflected itself in her novels.

Cather graduated high school and tired quickly of small town life. She moved to Lincoln in 1890. She wanted to enter the University of Nebraska, but her poor schooling in Red Cloud prevented her from getting admitted. She spent a year studying to enter college. She was admitted as a medical student, but abandoned that for the study of the classics. During her college years she became a dedicated writer on the classics. One of her literary papers was published, without her knowledge, in the Nebraska State Journal by one of her professors. She was enamored by the sight of her own writing published in a magazine. "What youthful vanity can be unaffected by the sight of itself in print!" she later wrote. The influence of prairie life made her stand out at the University of Nebraska. Many of the students would later remember her as unmannerly, masculine in appearance, and poorly dressed. After graduation, Ms. Cather decided to pursue a career in journalism. She moved to Pittsburgh, getting a job as a newspaper woman but she tired quickly of the hectic newspaper life. She moved to Allegheny, Pennsylvania, to become a high school teacher of English and Latin. She continued to write more consistently, and in 1903, she published *April Twilights*, her only volume of poetry. Shortly after that, she published *The Troll Garden*, a collection of short stories.

When she was 32, she moved to New York City and joined the editorial staff of *McClure's* Magazine. At *McClure's*, she edited and rewrote hundreds of magazine articles. Cather continued writing and publishing short stories in her spare time, in *The Century* magazine, *Harper's Monthly* and *McClure's*.

While doing research in Boston for a magazine piece, Cather met Sarah Orne Jewett, a sixty-year-old short story writer. Jewett advised Cather to become a novelist. "Your vivid, exciting companionship in the office must not be your audience," Jewett told her. "You must find your own quiet center of life, and write from that to the world."

Though she knew that her chances of becoming a successful fiction writer were slim, Cather resigned from *McClure's* after seven years. She traveled to the Southwest, where she became inspired to spend her life writing. She published her first novel, *Alexander's Bridge*, in 1912, and then her second novel, *O Pioneers!*, in 1913. Willa returned to the Southwest in the summer of 1915, and her third novel, *The Song of the Lark*, had its setting there in the ancient cliff dwellings of Walnut Canyon, Arizona. In 1918, Willa published *My Antonia* in which she returns to her childhood years in Nebraska.

After *My Antonia*, Willa continued to write novels set around characters from the prairie. She achieved popular success with *One of Ours*, which won the Pulitzer Prize in 1922. It is the story of a Midwestern farmboy who enlists in the army during World War I and is killed in France. The novel was based on a relative of Cather's, who died in that war. Her next novel, *A Lost Lady*, deals with the slow moral deterioration of a woman from a small Nebraska town. *The Professor's House*, published in 1925, is set in a small mid-western college. Of all her novels, she is best remembered for *My Antonia*.

The characters of Willa Cather's writings stem from the landscape of the prairie and her personal experiences growing up. Her early novels, including *My Antonia*, are reflections of the courageous immigrants from Europe who settled in the Midwest. Many of these immigrants could speak only their own native languages. They were people so poor they built their homes with almost no money, while braving the harsh prairie winters. Though many of the immigrants became successful farmers, many also lost their ambition and gave up. Willa saw, through their endeavors, what the pioneer spirit was all about.

Willa Cather died in 1947 at the age of seventy-three. Today, she is considered the definitive writer of the plains states, and one of the most acclaimed woman writers in American literature. Her tombstone, in the small town of Jaffrey, New Hampshire, bears a line from *My Antonia*: "That is happiness; to be dissolved into something complete and great."

Historical Background

When Willa Cather moved to Red Cloud, Nebraska in 1883, the United States was a nation growing in both geographical size and population. People from all over Europe were boarding boats headed for America and a new start. They were filled with the pioneer spirit, staking out pieces of farmland and calling them their own. First-generation Poles, Germans, Bohemians, Swedes, and Russians settled in the expanding Midwest to begin their lives again. They braved the harsh elements, penniless until their crops brought them economic relief. Cather's childhood experiences with these people served to capture her spirit for the frontier. They also defined human endurance.

When *My Antonia* was published in 1918, the world was in the aftermath of World War I. Willa began to see a nation in love with material things, and she felt the culture had become shallow because of this materialism. However, she also saw hope, through the selfless dedication of men and woman in their war efforts. She felt the importance of the pioneer spirit needed to be revitalized, and that is the message she wanted to convey when she wrote *My Antonia*.

My Antonia was immediately praised upon publication. One of the most immediate and important reactions to the novel dealt with Cather's use of the male narrator, a little-used device for woman writers at the beginning of the century. She was a pioneer in a sense, breaking new ground with her use of the narrator Jim Burden. Many critics have said that Jim Burden was really an autobiography of Willa herself. Other critics praised her ability to break away from the conventional form of the novel, noting that *My Antonia* was written in a series of dramatic or elegiac episodes out of the narrator's memory, conveying a nostalgic emotion. Harsher critics have viewed this nostalgic writing as "a devitalization of spirit," calling Cather's work too self-indulgent and claiming that she should have been writing about the life of her times, about life after the Great War.

My Antonia continues to be read and praised widely because of its universal appeal to a faith in humanity, of the rewards that come at the end of a long struggle. It has established Willa Cather as the most notable writer of the pioneer experience.

Master List Of Characters

Jim Burden—*Narrator, he has written down the memories of his friendship with Antonia. Jim is independent and courageous, with a love for adventure. When he returns to Black Hawk twenty years later, Jim is a successful lawyer in an unhappy marriage.*

Antonia Shimerda—*The eldest daughter of a Bohemian immigrant family of farmers in Black Hawk, Nebraska. She is forced to work as a servant on the farms of her neighbors after her father's death and goes on to live a weary but fruitful life with a large, happy family.*

Grandmother Burden—*A strong, hard-working, fifty-five year old Virginia-bred farm woman. She runs a clean, organized and cheerful home, and she is deeply religious. She takes care of Antonia after her father's death.*

Grandfather Burden—*Quiet, industrious older man, he runs the farm well, laboring in the fields along with the farmhands. He is a staunch Baptist. He is kind and loving to Jim and he helps out the Shimerdas despite their ungratefulness.*

Jake Marpole—*Accompanies Jim to his grandparent's farm in Nebraska. He is a Burden farmhand and he has a violent tem-*

per. However, he is well-received in Jim's memory. Jake leaves on a train after the Burdens move to Black Hawk.

Otto Fuchs—*Another farmhand, Otto is a skilled carpenter, and builds Mr. Shimerdas' coffin. He also keeps a trunkful of memorabilia from his adventures around the world. Otto leaves on the train with Jake after the Burdens move to Black Hawk.*

Peter Krajiek—*Bohemian who cheats the Shimerdas and forces them to live in poverty. Jake Marpole blames him for the death of Mr. Shimerda because Krajiek acts guilty after the suicide.*

Mr. Shimerda—*Father of Antonia, he is a kindly man who begins to despair over his family's poor condition and his failure to become a successful farmer. Mr. Shimerda never really wanted to come to America, and he becomes homesick for his native land and kills himself.*

Mrs. Shimerda—*Mother of Antonia, she is a mean and disagreeable person and has trouble grasping a new language. She complains about her poverty, and she envies the Burdens. She is greedy and materialistic.*

Ambrosch Shimerda—*Brother of Antonia, he is greedy and lacking in the social graces. He is also hard-working and religious, praying for his father after the suicide. He detests Antonia's child, and marries a domineering woman.*

Yulka Shimerda—*Antonia's younger sister, she is quiet and obedient to her parents. Later in the novel, she helps to raise Antonia's baby.*

Marek Shimerda—*Antonia's mentally afflicted brother that wants to show that he doesn't feel the cold weather. Later, Marek is sent to an asylum.*

Peter The Russian—*One of the two Russian neighbors whose story is told at some length by Antonia to Jim Burden. He is a friendly neighbor, a short man who is always smiling and shares his milk and produce with the Shimerdas. Peter looks after his brother until he dies.*

Pavel The Russian—*Brother of Peter the Russian, he becomes sick and tells his tragic tale of throwing a bridal party to the wolves. He is tall and thin, and he dies in his bed of tuberculosis.*

Mrs. Harling—*Born in Norway and the wife of a cattle merchant, she is stocky and ambitious, hires Antonia to cook for her household. She is an orderly woman, running a well-conducted household and working hard to keep things tidy. Her strong character has a positive influence on Antonia.*

Mr. Harling—*Christian is a grain merchant and cattle-buyer. He is a firm and serious businessman, and when he is home, the household revolves around him.*

Frances Harling—*Oldest of the Harling children, she is her father's business assistant, and he depends on her. She is a friendly and outgoing businesswoman, and she knows all the farm people well.*

Lena Lingard—*Daughter of a poor Norwegian farmer. She comes from a large family, and she is a beautiful, blonde girl with a low, sweet voice. She becomes Jim's companion in Lincoln, and she stays happily unmarried.*

Anton Jelinek—*Bohemian from Black Hawk, Jelinek visits the prairie after Mr. Shimerda's suicide to comfort the family. He is friendly and helpful, and he appears later in the novel running a saloon in Black Hawk.*

Mrs. Gardener—*Woman who runs The Boy's Home hotel, she is considered the best-dressed woman in Black Hawk, with a large fortune and many material possessions. She is fond of her diamonds, but is indifferent toward the rest of her riches.*

Blind d'Arnault—*Negro musician that comes to Black Hawk to play the piano. He is a happy person that tells the story of his learning to play the piano as a slave. Jim remembers him fondly.*

Ole Benson—*An unhappy farmer who falls in love with Lena and doesn't leave her alone.*

Crazy Mary—*Ole Benson's wife, she is jealous of Lena and chases her around the prairie with a knife.*

Anton Cuzak—*A good-humored Bohemian man who once lived the life of a fur worker in Vienna. He comes to Nebraska to visit his cousin Anton Jelinek, and meets Antonia. He marries her and lives a happy life on the prairie, fulfilling Antonia's dreams by becoming a farmer.*

Leo Cuzak—*Antonia's favorite child, he is an independent and brash twelve-year-old. He has a curly-head and he is handsome. He is jealous of his mother. He also plays his grandfather's violin for Jim and the others.*

Martha—*Antonia's first baby, who Leo Cuzak accepted before he married Antonia. Antonia tells Jim twenty years later that she married and moved away.*

Rudolph Cuzak—*Antonia's oldest boy, Rudolph arrives from the fair with his father. He tells the story of the Cutters at the dinner table.*

Jan Cuzak—*He is shy and often gets left out of conversations. His father brings him a paper snake from the fair.*

Ambrosch Cuzak—*One of the boys who Jim talks to in the haymow and helps with the chores.*

Yulka Cuzak—*One of Antonia's daughters, she helps her older sister with the chores and dances while Leo plays the violin.*

Anna Cuzak—*Oldest daughter on the farm, she cares for the little ones and helps her mother with chores.*

Wick Cutter—*A libertine and swindler who bickers continually with his wife over his money and who will inherit it. Antonia goes to work for him, and he plots a trip to her room to rape her. He commits suicide after murdering his wife.*

Mrs. Cutter—*A big, wild-looking, unhappy woman who paints flowers on china and bickers constantly with her husband. Her husband kills her to prevent her family from inheriting his fortune.*

Larry Donovan—*A train conductor and ladies man who convinces Antonia to move with him to Denver to become his wife, then leaves her when he is fired as a conductor for pocketing fares.*

Tiny Soderball—*One of the hired girls who works in the hotel in Black Hawk. Tiny moves to Seattle to start a boarding house, and eventually becomes part of the gold rush in Dawson City. She is an independent woman who winds up living in San Francisco.*

The Widow Steavens—*A tall, strong and independent woman who rents the Burden farm and recounts Antonia's life to Jim Burden on his return after twenty years.*

Gaston Cleric—*A Latin professor from New England with a dominating personality who persuades Jim to finish school. Cleric comes to visit Jim in his room and teaches him the classics.*

Colonel Raleigh—*Landlord to Lena Lingard, Raleigh is a southern colonel who falls in love with Lena. He gives her a black spaniel which she names Prince.*

Ordinsky—*The Polish violin teacher who lives across the hall from Lena Lingard who doesn't trust Jim when he comes to visit. Ordinsky is also in love with Lena, and she helps him with his torn waistcoat.*

Summary of the Novel

My Antonia takes the form of a memoir by the narrator, Jim Burden. In his memoir, Jim recounts the life of his childhood friend Antonia Shimerda, the eldest daughter of an immigrant family of Bohemian farmers living in Black Hawk, Nebraska. Antonia's father commits suicide and she is forced to farm the fields throughout her early teens. Later in her life she goes to work for the Harling family. She remains with the family until Mr. Harling interferes with her social life. Antonia then goes to work for the Cutters until Wick's amorous intentions cause her to leave.

Jim Burden enters a college in Lincoln, Nebraska, and leaves Antonia's side for two years. When he returns to Black Hawk, he learns of her failed relationship with Larry Donovan, the train conductor and ladies man who had promised to marry her. Donovan abandoned Antonia in Colorado, unwed and pregnant, and she returns home to Black Hawk, ashamed. She resumes her hard-working life in Black Hawk and gives birth to a daughter. After Jim goes East to attend law school, Antonia meets and marries Anton Cuzak, a fellow Bohemian, and has a large family with him. Content with family life, Antonia lives the rest of her days toiling and happy on her farm in Nebraska.

Estimated Reading Time

The average student should be able to read *My Antonia* in its entirety in a total of approximately 12 to 18 hours. It is suggested that the reading of the novel be divided into three blocks: Book I, *"The Shimerdas"* for the first block, Books II and III for the second block, and Books IV and V for the third block. These blocks divide the novel into the stages of Antonia's life, from her early childhood on the farm, to her life as a hired girl, and finishes with her family life as a mother and wife.

Block One-Book I: The Shimerdas

(Reading Time: 4-6 hours)

Block Two-Book II: The Hired Girls

Book III: Lena Lingard

(Reading Time: 4-6 hours)

Block Three-Book IV: The Pioneer Woman's Story

Book V: Cuzak's Boys

(Reading Time: 4-6 hours)

SECTION TWO

Book I: *The Shimerdas*

Introduction and Chapters 1-10

New characters:

Jim Burden: *the narrator, recounting his life in Black Hawk, Nebraska, and his memory of Antonia*

Antonia Shimerda: *a strong, healthy and intelligent Bohemian girl, whom the narrator meets in Black Hawk*

Grandmother Burden: *a well-ordered woman with whom Jim Burden goes to live*

Grandfather Burden: *a quiet and dignified old man with a white beard, wise in his ways*

Mr. Shimerda: *father to Antonia, he encourages her to acquire the knowledge she needs*

Yulka Shimerda: *Antonia's younger sister accompanies Jim and Antonia down to the river after they first meet*

Peter: *one of the Shimerdas' neighbors, an immigrant from Russia who is cheerful and generous*

Pavel: *Peter's brother, Pavel is a thin, sick man who confesses throwing his friends to the wolves as he lays on his death bed*

Summary

In the Introduction, the first-person narrator (perhaps Willa Cather herself) meets a childhood friend, Jim Burden, on a train ride through Iowa. Jim has become a successful New York lawyer and is trapped in a failing marriage, but he is able to recount with enthusiasm his childhood memories. On this train ride, the two old friends recall Antonia, a Bohemian girl they grew up with on the prairie, a girl they both remembered as a bright, energetic human being, in love with life. Jim announces to his old friend that he has been writing down everything that he remembers about Antonia. Months later, he brings his manuscript to the narrator's apartment. The manuscript is a rough draft, disorganized and without form, and Jim decides to title it *My Antonia.*

In Chapter One, Jim Burden, orphaned at ten years of age, makes the long train ride from his Virginia birthplace to his grandparent's farm in Nebraska. He travels the long journey with Jake Marpole, once a young farmhand of his father's. Along the way, one of the train conductors tells Jim of an immigrant family in the next car and encourages him to go meet them. One of the immigrants is a pretty, brown-eyed girl who speaks some English. However, Jim is too shy to go and introduce himself. Unlike the conductor, Jake displays a negative attitude toward the immigrants on the train.

The train arrives in Black Hawk at night, and Jim sees the immigrant family huddled around their possessions. He is then met by Otto Fuchs, a hired man who drives him to the farm. Jim rides across the dark, empty prairie to his grandparent's farm and worries about the immigrants survival.

Jim awakes in a small room on his grandparent's farm in Chapter Two. His grandmother takes him downstairs and gives him a bath. After his bath, Jim gets dressed and explores the house from the kitchen to the cellar. At the dinner table, he plays with the cat and gets to know his grandfather better. Jim eats dinner with his grandparents and Otto Fuchs, a hired hand from Austria, who has had many adventures in the Far West. Otto takes Jim out to see the horses in the stable, and shows Jim his pony. They talk about different places in the Far West.

The next day Jim goes outside to see the neighbor's sod houses and the tall grassy fields all around. His grandmother tells him about her snake cane that she uses in the garden and about the badger she's befriended. Jim finds a garden of pumpkins and asks his grandmother if he can stay there alone for a while. His grandmother complies, and Jim sits down among the pumpkins. There, he admires the peace and beauty of the country and begins to feel a deep connection to nature.

In Chapter Three, Otto Fuchs takes Jim and his grandparents to see their Bohemian neighbors and bring them provisions. They are the Shimerdas, the first Bohemian family to migrate to this part of the country. The Shimerdas speak no English and know nothing about farming. Their "house" is only a cave dug into the side of a small hill. They were cheated into buying the house and the land by a fellow Bohemian, Peter Krajiek, and they have no money left.

A woman and a young girl come out of the small house. The woman is trying to explain that her house is 'no good,' and Grandmother Burden consoles her. Jim notices the girl and her big brown eyes. She is the only one in the family who is cheerful. She is introduced as Antonia.

Mr. Shimerda comes out of the cave. Jim, Antonia and her sister run up the hillside and down to the creek. Jim tries to communicate with Antonia and teaches her some English words. Her father calls her to come home, and she and Jim run back to meet him. Mr. Shimerda gives Grandmother Burden a Bohemian and English alphabet, and asks her to teach Antonia English. Jim notices that Mr. Shimerda is unfriendly towards him.

Chapter Four begins as Jim takes his first long pony ride. Every day after this, he rides out to explore the country. He rides up the sunflower-bordered roads and through the cornfields to visit his German neighbors. He visits the big elm tree there, getting to know it like a person. Jim and Antonia later ride out to see the prairie-dog towns.

Jim begins to give Antonia reading lessons, and she helps Grandmother Burden in the kitchen. Jim notices that she is a good housekeeper. She in contrasted by Mrs. Shimerda's lack of domestic work and her complaining.

In Chapter Five, Antonia and her family make friends with their two Russian neighbors, Pavel and Peter. The men are strong and work hard to keep up their farm. Peter is a cheerful and helpful neighbor, and he communicates well with the Shimerdas. He is the only one home because Pavel is working in the fields. Pavel is a depressed and unhealthy immigrant. Jim visits the Russians almost every evening with Mr. Shimerda and Antonia. They all sit at the Russian's table and eat melons while Peter plays the harmonica. Peter later gives them milk and cucumbers to take home.

As we see in Chapter Six, Jim has been giving reading lessons to Antonia every day, and she has begun to speak English very well. She can talk to Jim about almost anything. She tells Jim about the badger, and how well regarded an animal it is considered in Bohemia. They watch some rabbits and Jim promises to make a fur hat for Antonia one day.

Antonia catches a grasshopper and puts it in her hair. At sunset, she and Jim head home. They notice Mr. Shimerda walking with his gun over his shoulder. Antonia tells Jim her father has been sick. They run to meet him, and Mr. Shimerda notices the grasshopper in Antonia's hair. Jim picks up the gun he has dropped and inspects it. Mr. Shimerda promises it to Jim when he grows up. Jim remarks that the Shimerdas are always giving their things away. Jim feels a deep pity for Mr. Shimerda. Jim goes home alone at sunset.

In Chapter Seven, Jim and Antonia borrow a spade from Pavel and Peter. They ride out to the prairie dog town to dig up one of their holes. They want to see how deep the holes go into the ground. Jim hears Antonia scream, and he sees a large rattlesnake curled before her. Jim crushes the snake with his spade. Antonia suggests they take the dead snake home as a trophy. Antonia rides home with Jim walking beside her with the dead rattlesnake. They show their prize to Otto Fuchs, who admires Jim for killing it. Though Jim realizes killing it was too easy and not much of an adventure, he leaves it hanging on the fence for all the neighbors to admire. It shows everyone that he "was now a big fellow."

Chapter Eight begins in late autumn. Pavel and Peter have run out of money and have begun to borrow heavily from Wick Cutter, a notorious money-lender from Black Hawk. While their debt grows larger and larger, Pavel hurts himself lifting wood one day and he

becomes seriously ill. Jim observes that bad luck seems to follow Pavel and Peter. One night Peter comes over to the Shimerdas, motioning that Pavel's sickness has gotten worse, and that he was afraid Pavel might not recover. Mr. Shimerda, Antonia, and Jim accompany Peter back to his farm to visit Pavel. Jim notices how sick Pavel has become. They hear the distant sound of wolves, and Pavel becomes frightened. Pavel then begins to speak for a long time in Russian, though Jim cannot understand him. Finally, Pavel falls asleep. On the ride home, Antonia tells Jim that Pavel told them a frightening story of the old country. She relates the story about a pack of wolves that attacked a wedding party on their sleds in the snow. Pavel and Peter, who were groomsmen for the party, pushed the bride and groom to the wolves in order to escape. They were the only two to survive, and they were run out of town.

Pavel dies several days after telling his story, and Peter sells everything he owns and leaves town. He goes to a construction camp to cook, and Jim and Antonia retell their wolf story to each other. The death of Pavel depresses Mr. Shimerda, who becomes more quiet and alone.

In Chapter Nine, Jim observes the first snowfall, and after the snow has packed on the ground, he drives around in the sleigh Otto Fuchs made for him. He rides over to the Shimerdas and gives Antonia and her sister Yulka a ride through the snow. They ride all day. At first they are happy and cheerful about the ride, but they become cold and miserable. They arrive home at dusk, cold from the wind in their faces. Jim becomes ill from this long sleigh ride.

Jim describes Otto Fuchs in more detail, and about his adventures out West. He recalls one funny story Otto told them of a woman he was traveling with on a boat who delivered triplets. Otto tells Jim how he helped her with her babies, and how he was blamed for her having them. Jim recalls the story adding to the warm atmosphere of his grandparent's house.

Jim and his grandmother visit the Shimerdas in Chapter Ten. They have not heard from them for several weeks, and they are worried. They take food with them, and Jim notices that the Shimerdas' cave is very dark and damp. Mrs. Shimerda falls to the floor crying at her family's poor conditions. Mr. Shimerda comes out from behind the stove and shows Jim and his grandmother the

holes in the wall where the girls sleep. Mr. Shimerda makes Grandmother Burden sit down, and he tells her that they are not beggars and promises to build a house in the spring. Grandmother Burden encourages them and gives them advice. Mrs. Shimerda cheers up and brings out a flour bag filled with strange brown chips. She gives a cup of these chips to Grandmother Burden. Antonia tells the Burdens that the chips were brought over from the old country, and that they tasted very good. Jim finds out many years later that the strange brown chips are dried mushrooms.

Analysis

From the introduction, we get the sense that the novel about to unfold is really a collection of personal memories. They are recounted in a narrative by the character Jim Burden. We also see that the memories of Jim's childhood are also the memories of Willa Cather's childhood. Ms. Cather has chosen to distance herself by working through the character of a male narrator. By distancing herself like this, she does not feel so close to any of the characters, and it becomes easier for her to narrate her story.

In the opening chapter, we get a brief glimpse of the Bohemian immigrant family, displaced from their homeland and huddled around their belongings. We also get a sense of Jim's awe of the land; his arrival at night and his ride across the black open prairie make him feel alienated and separated from his surroundings. We get the feeling that everything will be a struggle for the people settling on this land. Jim awakens to a life in a new land and a new home. In his grandparent's household, he begins to settle in, as he becomes familiar with his grandparents. When Jim visits the pumpkin garden, he is drawn in by the natural wonder of everything around him, and he develops a lifelong appreciation for the land. When he visits the Shimerdas the following day, we get a sense of the struggle that will take place: they speak no English, and they have no knowledge of farming. Ms. Cather is emphasizing the courage that embodies the pioneer spirit with her portrait of the Shimerdas. Their struggle will be long and difficult to make a life in this new land. We see the contrast of this struggle reveal itself in Jim's appreciation of the beauty the land has to offer, as he rides his pony through sunflower fields and rows of corn, and as he visits and "befriends" the solitary elm. The image of the tree, as a person one gets to know, will reappear later in the novel. It is also an image which relates directly to an experience in Ms. Cathers own life. From her memories of life on the prairie, she recounts the existence of a single tree as a monumental natural event. "Sometimes I went south to visit our German neighbors and to admire their catalpa grove, or to see the big elm tree that grew out of a deep crack in the earth...trees were so rare in that country...that we used to feel anxious about them, and visit them as if they were persons."

Jim and the Shimerdas meet their Russian neighbors, Peter and Pavel, and again Ms. Cather portrays the hard-working immigrant struggling to make it in a new land. The Shimerdas are able to speak with them, and we see their generosity revealed as they offer their fruits to their new neighbors and share their music. They are proud of their Russian heritage.

Jim begins to forge a friendship with Antonia, and she had learned English well enough to talk to him about anything. The grasshopper she catches in the field serves to evoke memories of her homeland. This evocation of memory is a pattern Ms. Cather repeats throughout the novel, mostly through her narrator, Jim Burden.

When Antonia mentions to Jim that her father has been sick, we get the message that Mr. Shimerda, like many other immigrants, is fighting a losing battle to survive in the new land. As he carries his gun across the field, we are warned of things to come.

Instead of telling her readers that Jim is growing into a man, we are shown it by his encounter with the rattlesnake. Like a medieval knight that has saved the damsel in distress (Antonia), Jim slays the snake, and like any proud warrior, he brings his trophy home to display his entrance into manhood. Again, this episode relates to the experiences Ms. Cather had as she grew up on the prairie. She recalled in her journals that her grandmother used a walking stick to frighten rattlesnakes away.

Part of the power of the pioneer spirit lies in the power of storytelling. This becomes clear in Chapter 8 in which the tragedy of the Russian neighbors unfolds. Jim's observation that the men are haunted by bad luck serves to tell us they had done something in their past to deserve it. When Pavel grows deathly sick and hears the howl of the wolves, his fear of death evokes his confession. He

tells a story on his death-bed of his and Peters' horrible ordeal in the old country while members of a wedding party. Pavel confesses how he and Peter had thrown the bride and groom off their sled in order to escape the attacking wolves; and consequently being shunned by the town for their immoral act.

The Russian story that Cather weaves into the narrative serves two purposes here: first, to evoke the sense of togetherness that comes from storytelling; second, to drive Mr. Shimerda into a deeper depression and toward his tragic destiny, as he relinquishes himself to a feeling of hopelessness.

The narrative moves forward with the change of seasons. The first snowfall on the prairie arrives, and Jim takes his sleigh out with Antonia to enjoy the wintry air. Again, Ms. Cather relates another story from the adventurous life of Otto Fuchs. This time we hear a humorous story to balance the tragedy of the Russians' tale. The light-hearted narrative gives the reader a sense that there is variety in the storytelling. The storytelling will act as a diversion from the monotony of life on the prairie.

Jim then visits the Shimerdas home after a two-week absence and finds their living conditions depressing. We get the sense that Mr. Shimerda has begun to isolate himself from his family as he appears from behind the stove. As Mrs. Shimerda breaks down and cries, we see the desperation that afflicts so many failing pioneer families struggling to survive. But the compassion that neighbors feel for one another reveals itself through Grandmother Burden as she consoles and cheers Mrs. Shimerda. Finally, we see another act of generosity revealed as Mrs. Shimerda offers her strange mushrooms to the Burdens. This offering serves as both an act of generosity and as a way to bridge the gap between their two very different ways of life.

Study Questions

1. Why does Cather have Jim Burden and the Bohemian immigrants arriving on the same train?
2. What is the significance of the train arriving at night?
3. Why does Jim want to be left alone in the garden?
4. To what does Jim compare the many-colored grasses on the prairie?

5. Why isn't Mr. Shimerda's fiddle of any use to him here?
6. What is the significance of the sunflower-lined roads?
7. Why does Jim visit trees "as if they were persons?"
8. Why does Cather choose to have the characters Pavel and Peter come from Russia?
9. Why does Cather have Antonia relay the tragic tale of the Russians to Jim?
10. Ms. Cather uses contrast to great effect in this section. Between what chapters do we see contrasts?

Answers

1. They are on a journey together, one that will ultimately forge a lasting friendship between Jim and Antonia.
2. Jim and the immigrants are strangers arriving in a new and savage land. The darkness emphasizes that they will have to struggle to make their way.
3. He feels a need for independence through his solitude with nature.
4. Jim compares the prairie to the ocean and its many-colored seaweeds.
5. Mr. Shimerda can't make money playing it the way he did at home, and he has become too depressed to make music.
6. Legend tells of Mormons throwing sunflower seeds on their journey west, leaving a trail for others to follow in their quest to worship God.
7. Trees are rare on the prairie, and his love of nature makes him consider all life sacred.
8. The Russian language serves as a means for the Shimerdas to communicate with their neighbors and because Russia is a distant, cold, and isolated country. This works to foreshadow the tragedy that will befall not only Pavel and Peter, but Mr. Shimerda as well.
9. To show that they are still both separated by language, and to begin to show Antonia's talent for storytelling.

10. We see contrasts between Chapters 3 and 4. The Shimerdas struggle to live on the land contrasting with Jim's pleasant pony rides through the country. In Chapters 8 and 9, the tragic Russian tale contrasts with Otto Fuch's humorous story. In Chapters 9 and 10, the Burden's warm and cozy house contrasts with the Shimerda's depressing cave.

Suggested Essay Topics

1. Why do all these immigrants risk their lives to leave their homelands and attempt to start over on a harsh prairie with little or no money?
2. Compare and contrast the lives of Jim Burden and Antonia. Explain what drew them together and enabled them to become close friends.

Chapters 11-19

Summary

In Chapter 11, on the first day of winter, a big snowfall hits the prairie just before Jake Marpole, the farmhand, is to go to town to Christmas shop. Jake is certain he can make it to town on horseback, but Grandfather Burden assures him he will never make it. Jim and his grandparents have a country Christmas "without any help from town." Jim and his grandmother gather together pictures and cards from around the house and sew together picture books to give the Shimerda girls.

Otto helps with decorations by making candles, and Grandmother Burden bakes candy and cookies. Jake goes out into the deep snow and brings back a Christmas tree, and Jim and his grandparents decorate it with gingerbread cookies. Otto reaches into his trunk and pulls out paper figures of all different shapes and images from the different places he has visited. He tells a little story about each and hangs them on the tree. Jim narrates he still remembers Jake and Otto sharing their country Christmas with him and his grandparents.

The peaceful holiday spirit continues in Chapter 12. Jim arrives downstairs in the kitchen on Christmas morning to find Jake and Otto returning from delivering Christmas presents to the Shimerdas. Jim stays inside and plays dominoes with Jake while Otto writes a letter. Mr. Shimerda arrives at the house in the afternoon to visit. He relaxes with the Burdens and seems content to be away from his cave. The Burdens invite him to stay for supper and he gratefully stays through the evening. Mr. Shimerda kneels down and prays in front of the Christmas tree, bowing down on the floor. Grandfather Burden accepts Mr. Shimerdas' religious ways. Mr. Shimerda leaves after dinner, he puts on his coat, lights his lantern and makes his way into the darkness.

In Chapter 13, the snow begins to melt on the prairie as the weather gets warmer. Mrs. Shimerda comes to visit the Burden's house for the first time. She sees how many things they have and thinks it is unfair. Out of pity, Grandmother Burden gives her one of her pots. Jim feels anger toward Mrs. Shimerda and toward all Shimerdas. Antonia doesn't think it fair that the Burdens have so much either. Jim feels little sympathy for their complaining, even when Antonia tells Jim how depressed her father has become. Antonia tells Jim her father misses the old country, and he doesn't play his violin any more.

Here we see another warning that tragedy is about to befall Mr. Shimerda. He has lost interest in music, which tells us that he feels no joy left in him. Without joy, their is no music in the heart. Mr. Shimerda is homesick for his native land. His friendships and popularity in Bohemia all came out of his playing the violin. Now, in a strange new culture, his violin becomes of no use. It has lost its appreciative value because his rich culture is now gone. Mr. Shimerda's violin, like himself, no longer serves a useful purpose.

Jim considers Ambrosch the most important and intelligent member of the Shimerda family, even though he is surly toward them all. Jim notices that Antonia treats him with utmost respect.

The weather stays mild and two of the farm's bulls get into a fight and begin to ram one another. Otto goes out to the corral and drives them apart with his pitchfork.

The biggest snowstorm in over ten years hits the prairie. Jake and Otto must shovel their way out to the barn and walk in huge drifts in order to feed the chickens.

In Chapter 14, Jim awakens one morning to the sound of excited voices in the kitchen. He goes down and sees Otto and Jake. Grandmother Burden sends Jim to the dining room and Jim notices Ambrosch asleep on the bench. Grandfather Burden pulls Jim aside and tells him that Mr. Shimerda is dead. Otto then tells them he heard a gun go off and then found him dead, how Mr. Shimerda went out to the barn after supper and shot himself there. Grandmother Burden can't understand why he would do such a thing. Jake believes that Krajiek, the dishonest man who sold them their house, had something to do with it. No one else believes that. They are all convinced it was suicide. Otto departs into the snow toward Black Hawk to bring back a priest and a coroner. Jim notices Ambrosch praying with his rosary. He prays for a long time, falls asleep, wakes up and prays some more. Jim has never seen this side of Ambrosch before, as he prays for his dead father's soul.

Everyone goes to help the Shimerdas, leaving Jim alone in the house. He feels important and gathers wood and eggs and does other chores. Jim feels the spirit of Mr. Shimerda in the house, remembering his contented face when he last visited. Jim realizes Mr. Shimerda died of homesickness, and he wonders if his suicide might have been prevented if he'd come to live with his grandparents. Jim thinks he might have been more content there.

After the family returns from the Shimerdas, Jake tells Jim about Mr. Shimerda's body frozen in the barn and the Shimerdas leaving it there untouched. Ambrosch is concerned about getting a priest to his dead father in order to save his soul. Jim quietly believes Mr. Shimerda's soul is still in the Burden household.

Chapter 15 begins as Otto returns from Black Hawk and tells everyone that the coroner is on his way. He also says that the priest who he was sent to bring back is on the other side of his parish a hundred miles away and won't be able to make it. The trains aren't running, so the priest cannot give Sacrament to Mr. Shimerda's body. Otto brings a Bohemian with him, a young man by the name of Anton Jelinek. Anton becomes concerned that there will be no priest arriving to save Mr. Shimerda's soul. He explains that suicide is a great sin in his country. He tells everyone that, as a boy, he helped a priest give the Holy Sacrament to dying men during the war. Anton feels a great sadness for the dead man and his family.

Anton ploughs the road leading to the Shimerdas. Otto uses

his cabinetry skills to build a wooden coffin out of some lumber scraps. As he builds it, he recalls the story of the last coffin he built for a man working the mines in Colorado. He tells Jim stories about other men he'd seen die.

Word of Mr. Shimerda's death spreads across the prairie. Many of the neighbors come to visit and share their condolences. No one is certain where Mr. Shimerda will be buried. Because it was a suicide, church graveyards will not take the body. Ambrosch and Mrs. Shimerda finally decide they will bury it on the corner of their property where a crossroads might eventually be built directly over his head.

In Chapter 16, Mr. Shimerda is buried on the fifth day following his death, because of the severe weather. Jim sees Antonia, who is mourning her dead father. The neighbors arrive on horseback for Mr. Shimerda's funeral. The men go to take Mr. Shimerda, now in his coffin, out of the house. They have to turn the coffin sideways to get it through the door, and the body comes partially out. Jim sees the dead body, and Otto nails the lid to the coffin. The men then take the coffin to the corner of the property and lower it into the ground. Grandfather Burden says a prayer over the grave, and Otto sings a hymn. Jim says he will always remember that funeral each time he hears the hymn.

Jim recalls years later, the crossroads that were built never crossed over Mr. Shimerda's grave, dividing it instead into a grassy island with the roads going around it. This is just as Grandfather Burden predicted. The grave remains untouched, which Jim attributes to God's kindness.

Spring comes to the prairie in Chapter 17. Some of the neighbors have worked over the winter to build the Shimerdas a new house, a four-room log cabin. The Shimerdas now have a windmill, chicken houses, and a cow bought from Grandfather Burden. Jim is now giving English lessons to Yulka, Antonia's younger sister. Jim notices how much Antonia has grown, and how she has begun to plough the fields every day. He suggests to Antonia that she attend school. She tells him she must work like a man now to help keep up the farm. Jim eats supper at the Shimerda's and begins to find them disagreeable, including Antonia. Grandmother Burden predicts Antonia 'will lose her nice ways' if she continues her heavy farm labor. Because she is working hard all of the time, Jim sees very little

of Antonia. Antonia works from sunup to sundown, proud of her strength. Ambrosch has assumed the role of head of the household, and he has plans to farm the land successfully. So he employs Antonia as a slave. She works hard only to please her brother.

Jim begins to attend the country school and sees very little of the Shimerdas in Chapter 18. He rides over to their house with Jake one day to get the horse collar Ambrosch has borrowed. Jake and Ambrosch have a dispute over the badly-used horse collar. They engage in a fight, and Jake knocks Ambrosch to the ground. Antonia and Mrs. Shimerda come running across the pond to attend to Ambrosch. Jim and Jake leave on their horses. Because of this incident, Antonia says she doesn't like Jim any more. Jim responds by saying he doesn't like her, vowing never to be friends again.

Grandfather Burden never holds a grudge towards the Shimerdas. When one of their horses gets colic, Antonia asks Grandfather Burden to help her. He helps the horse. Mrs. Shimerda thinks Grandfather Burden has come to take his cow back as payment and she tries to hide it. She is surprised to find he wants nothing for his services, and Mrs. Shimerda is grateful. Grandfather Burden restores the friendship to the Shimerda household, even though Mrs. Shimerda is still greedy and boastful.

In Chapter 19, summer comes to the prairie, and the corn grows wild. Jim and Antonia's friendship has been restored and now it is getting stronger each day. They go to the garden every morning to pick vegetables and talk. Antonia is working for the Burdens at this time, and her cheerful presence fills the house. Jim has been teaching Antonia English for some time now, and she can speak the language very well. Jim and Antonia climb up on the roof one night to watch a thunderstorm. Jim wonders to Antonia how sometimes she can be so nice, and other times so surly like her brother Ambrosch. Antonia tells him that life is hard for her, but that she will have to be hardened by life in order to survive.

Analysis

The second section of the first book opens with the first snowfall on the first day of winter. The Burdens and everyone else on the prairie are snowed in, cut off from the town. Through Jim's narration, we see the warmth and closeness that develops in rural

life through the celebration of a country Christmas. Even Jake and Otto become a closer part of the family. Jake cuts down a Christmas tree and brings it in.

Again, Ms. Cather weaves story-telling into the decorating of the tree, as the ornaments from Otto's cowboy trunk each has its own history and the tree, for Grandmother Burden, becomes "the Tree of Knowledge." Indeed, we could say that the decorated tree is a metaphor for the entire novel, an assortment of stories strewn over a natural backdrop.

In the midst of their cheerful holiday spirit, Mr. Shimerda arrives. He seems relaxed and content here, but we know he will ultimately have to return to his dismal cave, to the place that reminds him of his failure as a farmer. We can sense the air of death around him as he prays under the tree.

Mrs. Shimerda arrives to visit the Burdens for the first time soon after that. In contrast to Mr. Shimerda, who felt contentment in the Burden household, Mrs. Shimerda is bitter over their poor living conditions and doesn't think it fair that someone else can live so much more comfortably. She feels that the "wealth" should be shared, that the more others have, the more they should give. Grandmother Burden offers her one of her pans, though it is a gesture of pure pity. Jim wants nothing to do with pity, however. He tells Mrs. Shimerda how angry he feels about her actions. He later relates the incident to Antonia, and Jim pays little attention to Antonia's concern over her father's depression. The narrator becomes a fallible character here, showing us his blindness in not being able to see the importance of her concern.

A great blizzard hits the prairie, and it serves to foreshadow the coming of a tragic event. It also serves to contrast, once again, the beauty of nature and the struggle for survival in nature. Jim awakens one cold morning to find that Mr. Shimerda has committed suicide. The world has now become a much harsher place for the Shimerdas, especially Antonia. Jim ponders what might have been, if Mr. Shimerdas' prospects were a little brighter, this might not have happened.

Ms. Cather has set this tragic ending up from the beginning. We see the slow deterioration occur in Mr. Shimerda throughout the beginning of the novel, through his lack of music and his isolation. Without music and without the culture of the old country, there is no life left for Mr. Shimerda. He has gone against his wishes to stay in the old country only to appease his wife's wish to move to America.

Through this act, we get a sense that Mr. Shimerda, despite his resigned state of mind, is a compassionate human being. It is only fitting that he has played the violin, truly an instrument to symbolize the human soul. The instrument's ability to create both very happy and very sad music, in a sense, serves as a metaphor for Mr. Shimerda himself. As he prays beneath the Burden's Christmas tree, we get the sense that Mr. Shimerda's contentment is really a heavy veil for his disturbed interior. It is an ironic foreshadowing to his suicide.

Jim is left alone in the house after the suicide. Jim is not accustomed to an empty house. In the silence, Jim vividly recalls the last happy moments he shared with the tormented Mr. Shimerda. He remembers the man praying beneath his tree, so happy and content. Jim remembers him leaving in the night with his lantern and saying good-bye. In the haunting silence, Jim becomes certain Mr. Shimerda's soul has come back to rest in the house in a search for final contentment.

Ms. Cather has chosen this particular section of the book to emphasize the importance of religion, and religious differences, among the immigrants. The flight of Mr. Shimerda's soul becomes a primary focus here. Unable to fetch a priest, the Shimerdas are greatly concerned with the dead man's salvation. Anton Jelinek, a fellow Bohemian, shares their concern, remembering his experiences with a priest during the war, during which he saved the souls of many dying men. Through the introduction of a fellow Bohemian, we see that these people are deeply religious and superstitious. The deep sadness that hangs over them comes from the prospect that Mr. Shimerda, without the comfort of the Holy Sacrament, will not have his soul saved.

Again, we see the superstitions emerge when Mrs. Shimerda and Ambrosch insist the body be buried at the corner of their lot where a crossroads may be built. The image of the cross, of course, becomes implicit with the crossroads over the body. It would serve to take the place of the priest who never came. The Burdens can't

make sense out of this but bury the body with traditional prayer and song. We see the arrival of heretofore unseen neighbors, coming to pay their respects, attracted to the presence of death out of their collective curiosity.

Ms. Cather has the narrator take a step forward in time to show Jim's return to the grave site. Despite the tragic events leading to the burial, it is a most peaceful place for Jim years later, a place to remember. The crossroads were built across the land but never passed over the coffin, leaving Mr. Shimerda's body under an isolated patch of grass. This serves to symbolize his own isolated life, and the crossroads passing by his grave serve to symbolize the belief that his soul has not been saved, that Christ has "passed him by" and left him in the Purgatory of solitude. Jim, however, does not see this, instead believing that Mr. Shimerda, isolated on his island, finally feels at peace.

With spring comes rebirth, and we see it in the form of the Shimerdas' new log cabin. There is a rebirth for Antonia as well. She has grown considerably and has begun to assume much of the hard labor. Jim begins to see her uglier side through her physical efforts, as she becomes more like a man. She only works, and we see that begins to dull her. Jim sees the contrast when he sits with her on the roof watching a thunderstorm advance, wishing she should never have to work hard.

Study Questions

1. What is the significance of the snowstorm just before Christmas?
2. What is so unusual about Otto's trunk?
3. Why does Mr. Shimerda arrive at the Burden's alone?
4. What is the significance of the "false spring" just before the blizzard?
5. Name two places in this section where the narrator jumps forward in time.
6. When Antonia tells Jim of her father's worsening depression, why does he feel little pity for him?

7. On the morning of the suicide, how does Jim know that something has happened?
8. Why doesn't Grandmother Burden believe Mr. Shimerda could have killed himself?
9. What one thing makes Jake believe that Krajiek killed Mr. Shimerda?
10. How are Jim's and Ambrosch's concerns over the dead Mr. Shimerda related?

Answers

1. It cuts them off from the town and gives Jim a pleasant memory of a country Christmas.
2. Along with his boots and pistols, he keeps the delicate paper figures he takes out to decorate the tree.
3. Cather wants to reinforce his sense of isolation and loneliness.
4. It shows that there is "false hope" for things to get better, and things are going to change drastically.
5. At the end of Chapter 11, he jumps forward to say he'll always remember Jake and Otto that Christmas; at the end of Chapter 16, he recalls Mr. Shimerda's grave.
6. Jim is still angry at Mrs. Shimerda's wanting other people's things.
7. Jim hears excited voices in the kitchen as he awakes.
8. She always believed him to be considerate and that he wouldn't want the burden of his death on anyone.
9. Krajiek's axe fits the gash mark on Mr. Shimerda's face.
10. They are both concerned about the flight of Mr. Shimerda's soul; Jim believes it is in the house and wonders whether it will find its way back to the old country; Ambrosch is concerned it will not make it into heaven.

Suggested Essay Topics

1. Explain the significance of the seasons that come full circle from autumn to autumn in Book I.
2. Compare and contrast the relationship between Antonia and Jim in Section 1 (Chapters 1-10) and Section 2 (Chapters 11-19).

SECTION THREE

Book II: *The Hired Girls*

Chapters 1-8

New Characters:

Mrs. Harling: *neighbors to the Burdens in their new home in Black Hawk, she is stocky and ambitious. She hires Antonia as a cook*

Frances Harling: *oldest of the Harling children, she is an intelligent businesswoman who works for her father and helps the neighbors avoid Wick Cutter*

Lena Lingard: *a beautiful, blonde girl with a pleasant voice, she aspires to become a dressmaker and later becomes good friends with Jim*

Tiny Soderball: *friend to Lena Lingard, she is employed at a hotel, where the girls meet on Saturday nights. She appears later in the novel as her life story is told at some length*

Mrs. Gardner: *the best-dressed woman in Black Hawk who runs the Boy's Home Hotel*

Ole Benson: *a farmer who loves Lena and follows her around*

Crazy Mary: *wife of Ole Benson, she is jealous of Lena and chases her with a knife*

Blind d'Arnault: *blind Negro pianist who entertains Jim and the hired girls*

Summary

In Chapter One, Jim and his grandparents move from their farm and into the town of Black Hawk, at a house at the top of hill. Jim can see the river from the house, and he feels the river compensates for his loss of freedom. The Burdens rent their farm to Widow Stevens. Jake and Otto leave on a westbound train and Jim never sees them again. Jim and his grandparents begin to adapt to town life. Grandfather Burden becomes deacon of a church, and Grandmother Burden cooks church suppers. The Burden house becomes a stopping place for all of their old farm neighbors. Widow Stevens stops in and brings them news of Antonia. Grandmother Burden gets Antonia to work for their neighbors, the Harlings. Jim continues his farm-like mannerisms, and Mrs. Harling, their new neighbor, resents his actions and considers him savage. She forbids him to play with her children unless he behaves.

Jim describes life next to the Harlings in Chapter Two. Mrs. Harling, an energetic woman, is a mother to four children. Charley, Julia, and Sally are close in age to Jim. Frances is the oldest of the children and works as a chief clerk for her father. She is paid well, works hard, and has very little time to herself. Frances is a businesswoman who can handle herself, driving far out of town sometimes to help people in need and she helps them avoid the business practices of Wick Cutter. Wick Cutter is mentioned briefly in this chapter as having been outwitted by Frances and Grandfather Burden.

Mrs. Harling takes a ride to the Shimerdas and gets to know and like Antonia. She hires her as a cook for her household. Ambrosch argues that her wages should be paid over to him each month. Mrs. Harling and Grandmother Burden talk about how hard Antonia has worked.

When Antonia is hired at the Harlings in Chapter Three, Jim gets to see her every day and night. He often goes to visit her and the Harling family. Jim gets to know the Harling children better. He especially gets to know and like Nina and Charley, children closest in age to him. Jim notices there is a lot of noise and good cheer in the house when Mr. Harling isn't home. When he is home it is very quiet. Mr. Harling demands the attention of his wife. He is an arrogant man who sends the children off to bed early and spends a great deal of time at his desk. Most of the time he is not there, however, and the house is full of life. Antonia gets to know everyone in the household well. She develops a close friendship with Charley Harding and Jim envies her new preference.

In Chapter Four, autumn arrives on the prairie. The Harling children make popcorn and Antonia bakes a cake for Charley Harling. Lena Lingard comes to visit Antonia at the Harling house. She tells them that Tiny Soderball is working at the Boys Home Hotel for Mrs. Gardner. Lena is a pretty girl and she is nicely dressed. Lena explains that she has left the farm and has come to town to work for a dressmaker. Lena says she never wants to get married. She talks about dressmaking a little more and departs, asking Antonia to come visit her.

Jim narrates more detail about Lena Lingard and her family history. She lived in the Norwegian settlement, and her father, Chris Lingard was an unsuccessful farmer. Ole Benson lived at the edge of this Norwegian settlement with his wife, Crazy Mary, who was sent to an asylum for burning down a barn. Lena was becoming a woman and attracting the attention of Ole Benson, who began to follow her around. Ole's wife, Crazy Mary, noticed this and threatened Lena. She often chased Lena across the prairie. Mrs. Shimerda told Lena she had it coming to her for the way she flirted. Antonia feels cold toward Lean because of her reputation.

Jim begins to meet Lena in town to go shopping in Chapter Five. He goes with her to The Boy's Home, a hotel where Lena meets Tiny Soderball. Tiny is generous to Lena. They sit with the traveling salesmen and listen to Anson Kirkpatrick, a salesman from Chicago, play the piano. The salesmen are generous for Tiny's hospitality, and they lavish her with gifts.

Jim sees Lena Christmas shopping with her little brother Chris. Chris unwraps his presents and shows them to Jim. Chris wants to buy monogrammed handkerchiefs for his mother, and can't decide on "M" for mother or "B" for Bertha, her first name. He finally decides on "B." Chris gets on the wagon of a neighbors to go back to the farm. Lena weeps and says she gets homesick sometimes.

In Chapter Six, winter comes to Black Hawk, and Jim describes the town life that comes to a stop with the coming of cold weather.

Few people venture out and Jim walks the streets and lingers outside the church. Jim is bored living with his grandparents and he visits the Harlings almost every night. When he comes back from walking the streets, Jim notices the warmth and activity coming from the Harling household. He goes inside to see them, and plays charades and dresses up and dances with the Harling girls. Jim likes when Antonia tells her stories. She tells the story of a tramp that came up one day as she was working the fields. He was looking for work, and he climbed up onto a threshing machine and threw himself in. Antonia tells how she screamed and the men came running, but the man was dead. Nina Harling begins to cry and the family calms her down. Mrs. Harling scolds her for crying and doesn't scold Antonia. Jim notices the harmony between Antonia and Mrs. Harling, and how much they have in common. Antonia feels happier than she has ever felt living with the Harlings.

It is still winter in Black Hawk in Chapter Seven. Jim is more bored with the cold weather in town than he was living on the farm because there is very little to do. Jim goes down to the river with the Harlings. They skate and make fires. Jim is tired of school and winter, but the monotony is broken in March when Blind d'Arnault, a Negro pianist, comes to town. He gives concerts and visits the Boys Home. Mrs. Gardener, a well-dressed woman who runs the hotel, is out of town. Jim notices an unusual freedom in the hotel. Blind d'Arnault comes into the room. He is blind, but Jim notices that he has a happy face.

The blind man feels his way to the piano and sings Negro melodies. Jim relates Blind d'Arnault's history and tells of his early years on the slave plantation and how he became an accomplished pianist. The blind man plays the piano for them. Tiny, Lena, Mary, and Antonia are escorted into the room to dance with the men, and the girls waltz cheerfully to the music. Blind d'Arnault plays most of the night. Jim and the Harling girls thoroughly enjoy his company.

Spring comes and deepens into summer in Chapter Eight. A dancing pavilion comes to Black Hawk, and all of the children are sent to dancing classes by their mothers. Various vendors sell food outside the pavilion. Dancing becomes the most popular activity, and all of the girls in town wear their best dresses to the pavilion. Jim never misses a Saturday dance, when the tent stays open until midnight. Boys come into town from all of the farms in the area to watch the girls dance. There is a sense of the passage of time, and that things change quickly now.

Analysis

Willa Cather has divided her novel into several books for a reason: to establish a movement forward in time, and how that movement effects a change in the lives of each character. In Book II, we see that change at the opening of Chapter One, when Jim and his grandparents move from their farm into the town of Black Hawk. Here, their way of life will change tremendously. They will no longer have to work the fields. Instead, they will need to adapt to living in a town, socializing with more neighbors and getting involved in the community. The Burden household serves as a stopping place for many of their old farm neighbors. The location of their house at the edge of town shows us that Jim and his grandparents are not ready to let go of their farm lives, and they still want to keep in touch with their old friends.

With the introduction of the Harlings as the Burden's new neighbors, we begin to see that new friendships will be forged, and the reader will be introduced to many new characters. Indeed, the introduction of these new characters serves to replace the important people in Jim Burden's life. His grandparents are hardly mentioned from this point of the novel on, primarily because Ms. Cather wants to stress Jim's growth into manhood, and his movement into the world.

The Harling household serves as a stark contrast to the Shimerda home. Here at the Harlings, it is warm and pleasant. This sets the stage for a major change for Antonia, as she leaves both her farm life and dreary family life to come to work in town for the Harlings. Antonia grows to emulate Mrs. Harling, the mother that has raised so many happy children. Her emulation becomes a fortified glimpse into her own future family. Antonia's move to the Harlings also reinforces a continuing friendship with Jim Burden.

Jim is now growing into a man. He develops new friendships with the Harlings and also with Lena Lingard. Lena is a carefree girl who moves to town to become a dressmaker. She serves as a contrast here to Antonia, vowing that she will never marry, pursuing the life of an independent woman. Lena is a great deal like Jim, as Jim will eventually go off alone, like Lena, to seek his future.

Another important detail we should consider is Antonia's development as a storyteller. This development serves two functions: it reinforces Cather's theme of reminiscence that extends throughout the novel, and it establishes Antonia's mastery of the English language. With the story we get a pattern of changes that will signify change in Antonia's own life. She has moved from one culture to another, from a sad family to a happy family, and from country life to town life. Antonia is now able to relate all of the experiences in her life to an interested audience. It will set up her final choice in choosing between the two cultures in raising her family.

Dancing also becomes an important part of this section of the novel. It appears first within the Harling family and then with the Negro pianist at the hotel. Finally, it is brought to a full flowering with the arrival of the dance pavilion in Black Hawk. Jim sees the townspeople emerge and socialize in this final chapter. They work to earn money from the pavilion, and they send their children off for dance lessons. We also see the contrast begin to develop between the farm boys who travel to town for the dance on Saturday nights, and the town girls who wear their best dresses to the dance. This contrast is just another variation that Cather uses to establish the difference between country life and town life. It also reinforces the theme of music that runs throughout the novel. The music of the old country is taken from Mr. Shimerda in the first section, and causes his suicide. Now, the new experience of town life serves as a contrast to his loneliness. It brings the social life and the sound of music in the air.

Study Questions

1. Why does Grandfather Burden become a deacon of the church?
2. What became Jim's "compensation" for his lost freedom?
3. How did Ambrosch Shimerda take advantage of Antonia's reputation as a hard worker?
4. Why does Jim consider Frances Harling so important?

5. Why doesn't Antonia want to give all of her allowance to Ambrosch?
6. Why did Mr. Harling take Mrs. Harling away to their room on the west wing?
7. What is the significance of the traveling salesmen?
8. What is the significance of the altercation between Lena Lingard and Crazy Mary?
9. How are Antonia and Mrs. Harling similar?
10. What is the significance of the blind slave that becomes a pianist?

Answers

1. It establishes his involvement in the community.
2. Jim can see the river from the house.
3. Ambrosch hired her out to other farms.
4. Jim considers her important because of her independence as a woman.
5. Antonia wants clothes and pocket money.
6. They go there to discuss business.
7. The appearance of the salesmen emphasizes the idea of movement and change.
8. It shows that Lena is becoming a woman.
9. They are both strong and independent and don't try to imitate other people.
10. It serves as a metaphor: one must grope through the darkness to find one's desires.

Suggested Essay Topics

1. Discuss the contrasts that are being developed between the characters in this section.
2. Discuss the importance of independent women in this section, and why Willa Cather has chosen to develop these characters here.

Chapters 9-15

New Characters:

Wick Cutter: *the notorious money-lender of Black Hawk, always heard arguing with his wife*

Mrs. Cutter: *a wild-looking woman who bickers with her husband, busies herself painting china*

Summary

The men of Black Hawk are attracted to the country girls in Chapter Nine. The girls, transplanted from their farms into making livings in the town are more full of life. The town boys and country girls get together under the dance tent each evening. Even though the town boys aspire to marry town girls and settle down with their possessions, they watch the country girls with secret desires. They are especially attracted to Lena Lingard. The town boys see the life of the country in the hired girl's ruggedness and beauty. Despite their rugged beauty, though, the girls know very little of the ways of town life. They are much less refined than the town women, lacking in manners and proper refined speech. Their behavior stands in sharp contrast to the rest of the townspeople.

Antonia begins to be noticed at the dances in Chapter Ten. She comes in her finest dresses and she is one of the best dancers. Antonia has become obsessed with the dances and it is all she talks about. She is asked to dance often, and she is invited to parties and picnics. One boy, who is soon to be married, tries to kiss Antonia and she slaps him.

Mr. Harling warns Antonia not to go to the dances any more. He tells her she will have to leave the house if she goes. But Antonia wants to continue going to the dances, and she tells the Harlings she'll be going to the Cutters to work. Mrs. Harling warns her that if she goes to the Cutters to work, she won't be welcome back. Antonia explains that she has got to have her good times while she can.

In Chapter 11, Jim describes the character Wick Cutter, the moneylender. Cutter is a gambler and a businessman, often playing poker or conducting business in his office late at night. He is interested in horses, and goes out to the track to race in his buggy.

Cutter keeps his house and yard spotless, and nothing satisfies him. He treats women poorly, and he continually quarrels with his wife. Wick Cutter is mean-spirited in his exploitation of poor immigrants. He is greedy, and he cheats them out of mortgage money.

Mrs. Cutter is a big, wild-looking woman who always looks angry. She spends her time painting flowers on porcelain. She perpetually argues with her husband, from the time he comes home until late at night. They argue about everything, primarily about the inheritance of their property, and who will outlive the other, and whose family will receive the inheritance. They have stayed together because their arguing stimulates them.

Antonia goes to live with the Cutters in Chapter 12. She had become so obsessed with the social life, and now she cares only for dances and parties and picnics. She shops all the time for herself, buying clothes to wear to her affairs. She learns how to sew her own clothes from Lena, and she makes cheap imitations of the townswomens' dresses.

Jim Burden is now a senior in high school. He takes the girls, Tiny and Lena and Antonia, to the ice cream parlour, where they sit and talk. The dance tent leaves town, but the enthusiasm for dancing continues in the town as dances are given in various halls. Jim's mood has soured and he doesn't attend the dances regularly any more. Instead, he walks the streets or visits the drug store and the train depot, and he gets to know all of the houses of the town in his restlessness. He visits Anton Jelinek's saloon to listen to the talk of the patrons. Anton asks him not to come to the saloon any more because it will make his grandfather angry.

Grandfather Burden doesn't approve of the town dances, and sometimes Jim would sneak out of the house on Saturday nights to go to the dances at Firemen's Hall. It is the only dance Jim looks forward to. At each dance, Jim meets a variety of people who would arrive on trains from neighboring towns. The hired girls attended each dance as well. Jim would often dance with the girls, especially Lena and Antonia. Lena and Antonia are considered the two best dancers at the pavilion. Antonia begins to attend the dances with Larry Donovan the train conductor. When Antonia comes without him for one particular dance, Jim walks her home and requests a kiss from her. She refuses, and Jim tells her that Lena lets him kiss her and that he cares more for her than Lena. Jim quietly goes home. He remembers the dreams he would have after those dances about Antonia in the country. He remembers his most recurring dream of Lena Lingard in a short dress asking him to kiss her.

Jim notices his grandmother crying in Chapter 13. He finds out it is because he has sneaked off to the dances. Jim tells her there is nothing wrong with the dances and Grandmother Burden tells him she is crying because Jim deceived them. Jim promises not to go to the dances any more. He gets lonely without the dances and lingers downtown to walk Frances Harling home and talk to her about his plans after high school.

Jim graduates from high school and makes a commencement speech. He looks at Mrs. Harling while he is making his speech. Antonia is impressed with Jim's speech and tells his grandfather. She tells Jim she wished her father could have heard it. Jim tells her he dedicated his speech to him, and Antonia hugs him. Jim feels grateful and pleased that Antonia is so proud of him.

After his graduation in Chapter 14, Jim immediately begins to get ready for college, studying the classics and mathematics. He only has one break between his studies over the summer, when the girls invite him to a picnic down by the river. Jim goes there and reminisces about the times he spent there as a little boy. The girls arrive for their picnic, and Jim walks along the river to meet them. He finds Antonia crying. She tells Jim that the smell of the flowers has made her homesick for the old country, and it makes her think about her father's spirit returning there. Antonia tells Jim how different her mother and father were from one another, and how her father did not move to marry her mother. Jim promises Antonia that he will visit her country one day.

Jim and Antonia meet up with the girls. Tiny, Lena, Antonia and Jim sit and look over the town and talk about their parents' struggles to make it in this land. The girls talk about Selma Kronn, an immigrant who learned the language and went on to teach high school. The girls can't believe she is teaching because of the language barrier they all share and continue to struggle with. Antonia asks Jim to tell the story about Coronado and the discovery of the land. Jim tells the girls the history of how the Spanish first came to the land looking for the Seven Golden Cities. They left behind relics

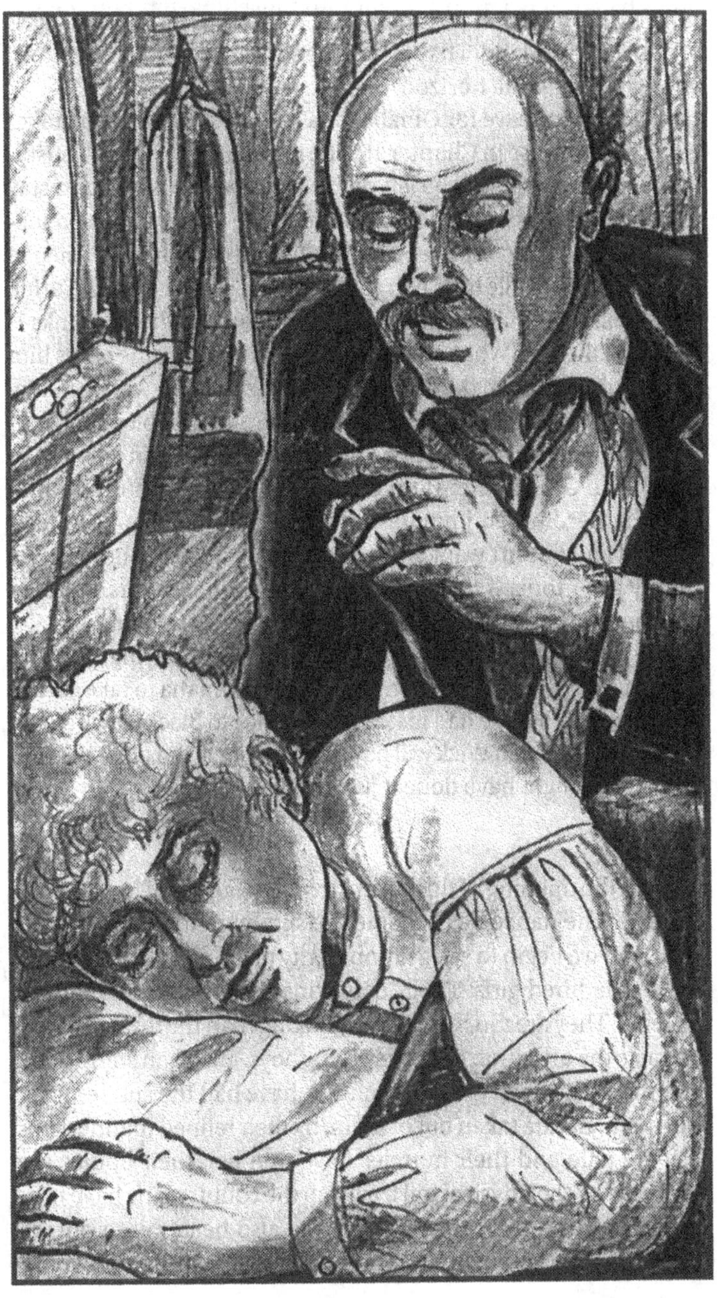

found by farmers and put them into museums. Jim and the girls look out over the land. They watch the sunset and the silhouette of a plough against the horizon.

The Cutters leave for Omaha for a few days, and Antonia takes charge of the house in Chapter 15. She is troubled by Cutters' suspicious actions just before he left on his trip, and she is afraid to stay in the house. She asks Jim to stay at the house for her, and he reluctantly agrees. Jim goes to sleep in Antonia's bed. He hears someone enter the house while he is lying in bed in the dark. It is Wick Cutter, who has slipped quietly into the house to ravage who he thinks is Antonia in the bed. When Cutter discovers it to be Jim, he grabs him by the throat in anger, thinking Jim is having an affair with Antonia. They get into a scuffle, and Jim punches him and runs bleeding from the house. He crawls in through his kitchen window and falls asleep on the sofa. Grandfather Burden finds Jim the next morning, and Grandmother Burden implores him to go to the doctor. Jim feels ashamed and doesn't want anyone to see him in that condition. He is angry at Antonia for asking him to stay at the Cutters. Antonia packs her clothes and moves out of the Cutter household.

Jim relates how Wick Cutter deceived his wife by saying he would have to stay overnight in a town on the way to Omaha to take care of some business, and he had instead come back to Black Hawk alone. Mrs. Cutter vows that Wick will pay for his actions. Jim observes that Wick Cutter might have done it just to anger his wife.

Analysis

With the opening of this section comes another of Ms. Cather's contrasts. The dance has become the summer attraction at Black Hawk, and we begin to see the popularity of the social life manifest itself in the hired girls. Their "countriness" works to both attract and repel. They are much healthier-looking than the town girls and it attracts the attention of all the young boys, and even some of the older men. The town girls, by contrast, have had the sun removed from them, nature taken out of them, by their refined mannerisms. They are pale and their muscles have thinned, their bodies less developed by the physical toil by which the country girls have been raised. However, the country girls have also been raised outside the mannerisms of town life. Their ignorance of proper town behavior becomes obvious to the townspeople. They are loud and carefree and lacking in the social graces by which the town girls have been raised. The townspeople, both men and women, consider them "a menace to the social order."

We see in Antonia, meanwhile, an obsession for these dances. Ms. Cather uses the dance as a metaphor here: dancing is a carefree affair in which you forget everything else. Antonia forgets everything and indulges herself completely in the social life, going to the dances without Mrs. Harling's wishes. When she is faced with the choice of maintaining a family life with the Harlings or an irresponsible life with the Cutters, Antonia chooses the latter. This decision weakens the friendship between Jim and Antonia because she is now socializing with other boys. Her move away from the happy family life of the Harlings also foreshadows a series of unfortunate events for Antonia.

Throughout this novel, Willa Cather portrays many of her characters not only by their actions, but by their physical features as well. There is no one more apparent in this aspect than the Cutters. They are physically repulsive people, and their appearance reflects each of their inner characters, and serves to set the stage for their ultimate demise.

Jim sneaks out of his grandparent's house to attend the dances. We see a contrast in Jim and Antonia, when he is caught doing this. While Jim sees nothing wrong with the dance, he feels ashamed about sneaking out and deceiving his grandparents. Unlike Antonia, Jim agrees never to attend the dances again.

Without the gay social life of the dance, Jim feels suddenly lonely. This signals a change that will occur in the narrator's life; he sees nothing left in the town to keep him here. Without the dance, and the continued strength of Antonia's friendship, there is no choice but to move on.

Jim graduates high school and gives a stirring commencement speech that surprises Antonia. She realizes through his thoughtful speech that he is destined for better things. Jim begins to study for college, which signals the beginning of a change of life for him. It also signals the closing of this section of Cather's novel.

Just as Ms. Cather weaves a series of contrasts throughout the novel, she also uses the power of reminiscence. This power is used

to great effect in the scene by the river, when Jim meets the girls for a picnic. It is his last carefree time with them before he goes off to college, and that triggers a series of reminiscences by each character. The girls' memories are tied to their homelands and their great struggles to make it in the new land. Jim's story about the Spaniard discovering the land serves to weave a history through all of it. Finally, the silhouette of the plough against the setting sun says everything that words cannot, symbolizing, for one awesome moment, the pioneer spirit.

Antonia's decision to live with the Cutters comes back to haunt her with Wick Cutter's attempted rape. Just as Willa Cather uses the narrator, Jim Burden, to remove herself from the work, she uses Jim to remove Antonia from the scene of the attempted rape. Jim agrees to sleep in the Cutter household, and Wick sneaks into the room in the dark to ravage Antonia. Jim is hurt in the ensuing scuffle, and he is angry at Antonia. This is an immature reaction on Jim's part, signaling that he will need to get out of this small-town life in order to become a man.

Study Questions

1. Why did Jim want Lena to settle down with a town boy?
2. What reasons does Antonia give for wanting to work for the Cutters?
3. How did Wick Cutter say he got his start in life?
4. Under what condition does Mrs. Cutter threaten to leave Mr. Cutter?
5. Who does Jim compare to Snow White?
6. How does Tiny Soderball make Jim angry?
7. Who was the proprietor at the saloon that Jim visits?
8. Who does Jim consider "a professional ladies man?"
9. As Jim gets more lonely, who does he find for companionship?
10. Down by the river, with whom does Jim remember hunting?

Answers

1. To give all the country girls a better reputation in the town.
2. They pay more, they have no children, and the work is easy, giving her more free time.
3. Wick got his start by saving the money other men spent on cigars.
4. If he chopped down the cedar trees around the house and took away her privacy.
5. Antonia is compared to Snow White.
6. She tells the girls she heard that Jim's grandmother wanted to make him a Baptist preacher.
7. Anton Jelinek, the Bohemian who visited the farm during Mr. Shimerda's death.
8. Larry Donovan is a "professional ladies man."
9. The telegrapher and the cigar-maker and his canaries.
10. Jim remembers hunting with Charley Harling.

Suggested Essay Topics

1. Discuss the differences Jim sees between the country girls and the town girls.
2. Explain the importance of the dance pavilion to both Jim and Antonia.

SECTION FOUR

Book III: *Lena Lingard*

Chapters 1-4

New Characters:

Gaston Cleric: *Jim's Latin teacher at college who inspires him to read the classics and go to law school back East*

Colonel Raleigh: *Lena Lingard's landlord, Raleigh gives Lena a dog and falls in love with Lena*

Ordinsky: *the Polish violin teacher who lives across the hall from Lena and is also in love with her*

The Widow Steavens: *a tall, independent woman who has rented out the Burden farm and tells Jim all about Antonia*

Larry Donovan: *the passenger conductor who promises to marry Antonia and then leaves her pregnant and alone*

Summary

The section opens with Jim attending college in Lincoln, Nebraska. Gaston Cleric, his Latin teacher, becomes his mentor and introduces him to the world of literature. Gaston is often spouting poetry. When Jim rents a small room to live in and study, Gaston comes to visit him and talk about poetry. Jim thinks Gaston could have been a great poet if he had chosen not to teach. Though Jim

admires the scholarship of Gaston Cleric, he realizes he will never be able to become a scholar like him. Jim relaxes from his studies to reminisce about simpler times.

In Chapter Two, Jim reads a line from Virgil that means 'the best days are the first to flee.' Jim remembers the history Gaston Cleric had told him about Virgil's dying days. Jim leaves the classroom and goes back to his room to think about Virgil. Jim hears a knock at the door, and opens it to see Lena Lingard, who has come to visit him. Lena tells him she has opened a dressmaking shop in Lincoln. She is well-dressed and proper now, and Jim remembers back to when she ran barefoot on the farm. Lena tells Jim about Antonia and her engagement to Larry Donovan. Jim narrates that he never liked Larry Donovan. Lena suggests that they go to a show together sometime. Then she leaves, promising to keep in touch. Jim remembers his days with the hired girls and his dreams of Lena. Then he remembers the Latin line from Virgil, and he connects his memory of the hired girls with the poetry he has learned.

Chapter Three begins in early spring, and Jim often goes to the theater with Lena to see a variety of plays. He describes in more detail the night he and Lena go to see "Camille." They are both very excited with the rise of the curtain, and Jim sees lavishly decorated people and things on the stage. They notice that the lead actress is old and lame while the male hero of the play is young and handsome. Jim knows the actors on the stage well, and he and Lena share the vicarious experience of the drama that unfolds. Lena weeps throughout the play, and Jim is proud to have brought her instead of one of the less appreciative Lincoln girls. He and Lena leave in the rain under Jim's umbrella. This is a memorable moment for Jim, and he is proud of Lena, and respects her as an independent woman.

Jim describes the life of Lena the dress-maker in Chapter Four. He notices that she seems cut out for her profession, fitting people into fashionable clothes and getting along well with her customers. She is also a very good businesswoman, and she makes good money. Jim walks Lena home from her shop after his classes. He has Sunday breakfast with her at her apartment. A Polish violin teacher lives across the hall and disturbs Lena's dog with his rehearsals. Old Colonel Raleigh, her landlord, had given her the dog. Lena is very fond of the dog, and it can do many tricks.

Jim respects Lena's mastery of the English language and notices she has picked up many of the local expressions. Jim visits her in the mornings and he notices her beauty in the light. He remembers Ole Benson's reaction to her beauty back in his farm days, and now he can understand it. Lena shares her detailed memory of Ole Benson. She tells Jim about his hardships coming to the new land and all of his misfortunes along the way. When Jim stays late at Lena's, Ordinsky the Polish violin teacher comes out as he is leaving. The man disapproves of Jim's late visits. Old Colonel Raleigh, Lena's landlord, is good to her and fixes her apartment to her liking. He is a widower who finds Lena appealing and falls in love with her. The colonel gives Lena his black spaniel. Mr. Ordinsky, the violin teacher, also falls in love with her. Ordinsky comes over one night to ask Lena to repair his torn waistcoat. She takes the coat into the next room to sew it, leaving Mr. Ordinsky and Jim alone in the room. Mr. Ordinsky expresses his lack of respect for Jim. Jim explains to him that he and Lena have been friends since childhood, and Mr. Ordinsky apologizes for his behavior. Ordinsky is friendly to Jim after that and he asks Jim to take an article he has written to the newspaper.

Jim goes to Lena's apartment often and has begun to neglect his studies. He visits and gets to know her dog and the violin teacher. Jim notices that he, Mr. Ordinsky, and the landlord are all in love with Lena.

Gaston Cleric comes to visit Jim after he is offered a job at Harvard College. Cleric advises Jim to follow him to Harvard and not to involve himself with Lena. Cleric writes to Grandfather Burden expressing his desire to take Jim with him. His grandfather agrees. Jim goes to visit Lena again. He tells her that he will be leaving for college. She asks Jim why he must go, and asks whether he thinks she has been good to him. She explains that she became close with him because Antonia had warned her to stay away from him, and that she doesn't want to hold him back. Lena tells Jim she doesn't want to marry. She says she would rather stay single and lonesome. Lena explains that her childhood involved a great deal of hard work caring for a family, and she wishes never to repeat it. Jim tells Lena he is going east to attend Harvard with Gaston Cleric. He visits his grandparents, goes to Virginia, and then moves to Boston at nineteen to go to college.

Analysis

In "Lena Lingard" we again see Cather's use of contrast worked to great effect. This contrast first presents itself through Jim's studies. Where he had once listened to the simple stories of the land and its people, Jim now tries to comprehend the stories that are literature. He works hard to understand the Latin terminology and the meaning imposed by Virgil's long passages, and he tries to understand and embrace the poetic outbursts of Gaston Cleric. This is also another instance of Ms. Cather's life projecting itself into the novel. Cather entered the University of Nebraska intent on becoming a doctor, and was influenced by the classics to pursue a career writing.

Jim Burden realizes he will never become a scholar like Gaston Cleric, mostly because his past has shaped such strong and simple memories. Remembering the people and the powerful stories out of his past is much more valuable to his life than the memorizing of any literary passage. It becomes a choice of memory over memorization. It is ironic that this realization comes from Jim's reading of a line from Virgil, "Optima dies...primus fugit." The line means that the best days are the first to flee, and awakens in him the realization that the simpler times have passed him by. Jim can now only bask in their memory. The line also tells us that Jim is maturing and striking out into the world with more responsibility.

We see this maturity manifested with the arrival of Lena Lingard. She is an independent women who has struck out on her own as a dressmaker. She visits Jim to reinforce the connection to his past, telling him about the exploits of Antonia and Larry Donovan. Ms. Cather, we might note, also uses the character of Lena to keep the connection to Antonia close, so that throughout this section we are kept aware that the narrator and Antonia will be reunited in friendship. The connection to Jim's past is also solidified when he remembers his dreams of Lena in the fields. This image makes him remember the line from Virgil.

When Jim and Lena go to the plays together, we see his maturity begin to develop. Again, the contrast in story-telling unfolds in Jim's description of the play "Camille." Here we see the story unfold on the stage through Jim's narration and intricate description of the lavishly decorated set and the development of the play itself in all its classic glory. Pitted against this comes the weeping of Lena. Jim respects Lena's emotional outburst, for it serves to illuminate for Jim the vast difference between the impersonal story of "Camille" and the very personal memories of his boyhood. It also serves to show Jim's maturity; he is grateful that Lena appreciates the play and that he has not brought "some Lincoln girl" who would not appreciate the beauty of a well-told story.

As a further test of Jim's maturity, he must make the decision to break the ties to his past. He has begun to forge a deeper friendship with Lena and her neighbor, and he is being drawn away from his studies. Gaston Cleric, much like Virgil, acts as Jim's guide. He advises Jim to continue his education at Harvard. This will require Jim to break his strong bond with Lena. Jim makes the mature decision to do this, closing another part of his life into memory.

Study Questions

1. Why did Gaston Cleric move west?
2. What was so unsusal about Jim's room in Lincoln?
3. What does Jim believe was "fatal" to Gaston Cleric's "poetic gift"?
4. Why did Lena insist on paying her own way to the theatre?
5. What did Lena plan to do with the money she saved?
6. Where does Lena tell Jim Antonia is working?
7. What does Jim remember when he hears Lena laugh?
8. Why was Jim puzzled by Lena's business success?
9. What was the significance of the umbrella Jim uses on his way back from the theatre?
10. Why does Lena like to be lonesome?

Answers

1. Gaston's doctor suggested he move west in order to improve his health.
2. The small room was once a linen closet.

3. Jim believes Gaston's "bursts of imaginative talk" prevented him from becoming a great poet.
4. She insists on paying her way because she was making good money and Jim was a student with little money.
5. She wants to build a house for her mother.
6. She is working at the hotel for Mrs. Gardener.
7. It makes Jim remember the laughter of all the hired girls.
8. Jim was puzzled because most business people are hard-nosed, but Lena is an easy-going person.
9. It was the present Mrs. Harling gave him for his graduation.
10. When she was a young girl, she never had time to herself.

Suggested Essay Topics

1. Explain why Willa Cather has chosen to devote one of the books of her novel to Lena Lingard.
2. Discuss the importance of the narrator leaving Black Hawk for college life.

SECTION FIVE

Book IV: The Pioneer Woman's Story

Chapters 1-5

Summary

In Chapter One, Jim returns to Black Hawk for the summer after finishing his pre-law schooling at Harvard. On his first evening back, Mrs. Harling, Frances and Sally come to visit him. Frances Harling tells him all about Antonia and how Larry Donovan deserted her and left her alone with her baby. She just works hard for her brother Ambrosch now. Jim is disappointed with Antonia when he hears of her misfortune. He doesn't think it is right after seeing Lena's good fortune.

Jim narrates his relationship to Tiny Soderball. He recounts the events leading to her good fortune, from her job running the sailor's lodge to her trip to Alaska in search of gold. Jim recalls her good luck founding the gold-mining town of Dawson City in the Yukon, where she meets a Swede whose legs have been frozen. Tiny and the Swede become friends because they both speak Swedish and like to make money. When the Swede dies, he leaves Tiny his fortune. She becomes interested only in money after that and invests her money to amass an even greater fortune. Tiny goes to live in San Francisco, and she tries to persuade Lena Lingard to move west and go into business with her. Because of her infatuation with money, Lena is Tiny's only friend.

When Jim goes to get a photograph taken with his grandparents, in Chapter Two, he notices a picture of a baby on the wall. The photographer tells him that the baby belongs to Antonia. The picture makes him want to go visit Antonia again. Jim remembers Larry Donovan the passenger conductor and his friendly gestures toward all of the women boarding the trains. Jim wonders why Antonia married such a man and he wants to find out how Antonia's marriage fell through. He talks to Mrs. Harling and tells her he would like to find out more about Antonia's misfortune. Mrs. Harling tells Jim to go see the Widow Steavens. She tells him that the Widow Steavens has forged a close friendship with Antonia, and she would know everything that has happened in the passing years.

Jim arrives at the Widow Steavens' in Chapter Three. He notices how much more the land and the buildings on the farm have become enriched. The Widow Steavens comes out of the house to meet Jim. He tells her he has come to find out all about Antonia. The Widow Steavens invites Jim to stay the night and cooks him supper. After supper they sit down upstairs, and she tells him about Antonia, how Larry Donovan had asked her to move to Denver and everyone had helped make things for her new home. After she moved there, Widow Steavens explains to Jim, she lost touch with everyone until she returned after a month. That was when Antonia told the Widow Steavens that she wasn't married and Larry Donovan had left her. She explained that Larry was fired as a conductor, and when he ran out of money, he left in shame. The Widow Steavens compares Antonia to Lena. She tells Jim how Antonia is a much better person, and that she didn't deserve the disgrace that has befallen her. She tells him that Antonia just worked in the fields now and that she had become quiet and unsociable. Ambrosch encourages Antonia to continue laboring in the fields. He rejects the Widow Steavens when she tells Ambrosch that he is working Antonia too hard. He suggests to Antonia that she not visit any more. The Widow Steavens saw Antonia becoming weary and lonely. One day, she tells Jim, Antonia went into the house and delivered her own baby. The Widow Steavens explains to Jim that she has forged a strong friendship with Antonia, and that she continues to help Antonia raise her child. Ambrosch wanted to drown the baby when he first saw it, but the Widow Steavens threatens harm to him if anything happens to the baby. She tells Jim that the baby is well cared for, and she tells him that she wishes Antonia would get married and raise a family.

Jim sleeps in his old bedroom that night, and reminisces about his memories of the prairie.

Jim goes to visit Antonia in Chapter Four. Yulka, Antonia's younger sister, shows Jim the baby. He goes out into the fields to meet Antonia while she is working, and notices though she is much thinner, she still looks very healthy. Jim walks out to her father's grave site with her. He sits down with her and tells her about his experiences at law school, about his studies and about the death of his mentor Gaston Cleric. Jim tells her that he will be going away, and how much a part of his life she has become. They walk back at sunset across the fields and Jim reminisces about being a little boy again. He promises Antonia that he will always remember her.

Analysis

In "The Pioneer Woman's Story" we see Jim's return to Black Hawk. He learns through Frances Harling of Antonia's misfortune with Larry Donovan. Ms. Cather plays on the idea of fortune in this book; she has her narrator, Jim Burden, contrast the very different fortunes of the hired girls. Jim recounts his close friendship with Lena and finds her independent lifestyle disturbing after hearing of Antonia. Jim then recounts in detail the uncanny fortunes of Tiny Soderball. The narration of Tiny's life serves two functions at this point of the novel: it contrasts against Antonia's failed marriage, and it reinforces, once again, the power of storytelling.

It is important to note Cather's decision not to have Jim go directly to Antonia upon his arrival at Black Hawk. In order to be true to the underlying theme of storytelling that runs through the novel, Jim will hear Antonia's unfortunate story told to him. Jim calls on the Widow Steavens to relate the events of Antonia's failed marriage. It is important to note that Antonia and the Widow Steavens have become good friends. This serves as a foreshadowing of events in Antonia's life, her return to the land.

The theme of reminiscence is solidified at the end of this section when Jim visits Antonia. Like so many times before, they walk through the fields at sunset, symbolizing the close of another event in their lives into warm and unforgetful memory.

Study Questions

1. Where does Frances Harling tell Jim that Antonia is living?
2. What happened while Tiny Soderball was running her boarding house in Seattle?
3. What was the only thing that now interested Tiny?
4. Why did Tiny limp when she walked?
5. What does Jim notice about the picture of Antonia's baby?
6. Why was Larry Donovan fired as a passenger conductor?
7. How did Larry Donovan treat his female passengers different from his male passengers?
8. What does Jim notice about the old pasture lands?
9. Who was in the basement when Mrs. Steavens and Jim went into the sitting room?
10. Who shows Jim Antonia's baby?

Answers

1. Antonia has gone back to live on the farm.
2. Gold was discovered in Alaska.
3. Tiny was only interested in making money.
4. She lost some of her toes in the cold weather.
5. The picture is in a great gilt frame.
6. He was blacklisted for knocking down fares.
7. He was cold and distant toward the men and friendly toward the women.
8. It is being broken up into wheat fields and and corn fields.
9. Mrs. Steavens' quiet brother was sitting in the basement reading his farm papers.

10. Yulka Shimerda shows Jim the baby.

Suggested Essay Topics

1. Compare and contrast Tiny Soderballs' and Lena Lingard's success with money.
2. Discuss the reasons why Willa Cather chose to have Antonia return to the Shimerda farm as an unwed mother.

SECTION SIX

Book V: *Cuzak's Boys*

Chapters 1-3

New Characters:

Anton Cuzak: *Antonia's husband, he is kind and loving and he brings gifts to his children*

Rudolph Cuzak: *Antonia's oldest son. He tells the Cutter story to Jim in great detail*

Leo Cuzak: *the most mischievous of the Cuzak family, he is also Antonia's favorite child*

Ambrosch Cuzak: *one of the boys who Jim befriends. He helps his brother Jan bury their dead dog in the orchard*

Jan Cuzak: *Jan is little and shy, and rarely talks during family conversations. He cries when the dog dies on the side of the road, and his father brings him a paper snake from the fair*

Martha: *Antonia's oldest, who is married and lives away from the Cuzak farm*

Anna Cuzak: *the oldest daughter on the farm, she cares for the little ones and helps her mother with the chores*

Yulka Cuzak: *Yulka helps Anna care for the little ones, and she dances for Leo when he plays the violin*

Summary

In Chapter One, Jim leaves Black Hawk and doesn't return for twenty years. He has had little contact with Antonia and Jim learns that she has married a Bohemian man by the name of Cuzak, and that they have had many children. He also finds out that she is poor. Jim is reluctant to visit her. He thinks it will mar many of their pleasant memories. He meets with Lena Lingard and she urges him to go visit her. Jim takes the train to Nebraska to visit Antonia and her family. He drives through the open country to the Cuzak farm. Jim notices two boys kneeling over a dead dog and they are crying. He finds out they are two of Antonia's sons. They follow him up to the farmhouse and open the gate for him. Another boy runs out to tie up Jim's horses and Jim notices another curly-haired boy climbing up the windmill. Jim notices ducks and geese and cats running about the farm. The boys invite him into the house and he sits at the table. Antonia comes into the room and doesn't recognize him. She thinks he is a businessman and tells Jim that her husband and her oldest son are away at the fair. After Antonia recognizes him, they embrace and then she gathers her children together to introduce Jim. They have all heard a great deal about him from their mother's stories. The children have an immediate respect for Jim. Antonia tells Jim that she has brought her children up speaking mostly Bohemian. She plays with the children and talks about each of them. She tells Jim that she loves Leo, the most mischievous of her children, best of all. Jim notices that Antonia has lost most of her teeth, but that she is still a robust woman.

The children take Jim out to show him their fruit cave. It is a small cave surrounded by hollyhocks with barrels inside. The boys show Jim the spiced plums they have stored in the barrels, something Jim has never seen. On the way back from the fruit cave, Jim notices the beauty of the Cuzak's farmhouse with all of the surrounding orchards. He and Antonia walk through the orchards, and Antonia tells Jim how much she loves trees. Antonia tells Jim how she planted the orchard and took special care of it, caring for each tree as if they were each one of her children. In the grape orchard, the boys find a clearing where they want to bury their dead dog. Jim and Antonia sit and watch them, and Jim feels peaceful. Jim reminds her about the quail they once hunted. Antonia also tells Jim about her husband,

and how hard they worked to make a happy family. She tells him about her oldest daughter Martha, and how she married and had a baby. In the peacefulness of the orchard, Antonia explains that motherhood has given her a respect for life. She tells Jim that her strength enabled her to survive, and that she passed that strength on to her children. Jim tells Antonia she should never have left the farm to live in Black Hawk, but Antonia disagrees with him. She tells him that despite her love for the country, she is grateful for her town-life experience. She says that the experience of life with the Harlings taught her to bring her children up much better.

Jim goes to sleep with the Cuzak boys in the haymow. He feels younger in the boy's company, and he helps them to milk the cows. Jim tells them that he was once in love with their mother, something they never knew. At the dinner table the next night, Antonia sits at the head of the table surrounded by Jim and her family. One of the boys play the violin while the girls dance. After dinner, Antonia brings out a box of photographs to show Jim. Her children lean over them as she shows Jim pictures of her wedding and then pictures of Ambrosch, the Harlings, and a tintype of Jake and Otto, and the picture reminds them of the coffin that Otto built. Antonia recounts the memories from the other photographs, of the Bohemian Marys, Frances in her riding costume, and a recent photo of Lena. Jim tells Antonia that Lena still looks the same.

Jim goes to the haymow with the boys for the night. The boys immediately go to sleep, but Jim lies awake and thinks about his memories of Antonia.

In Chapter Two, Jim awakens with the boys in the morning and they all go to breakfast. He watches the older boys go off to work the fields. A wagon drives in with Anton Cuzak, Antonia's husband, along with her oldest son. Jim has immediate respect for him. The oldest son describes the fair they had been to see. Anton brings out several gifts he has bought at the fair and gives them to each of his children. At the dinner table that evening, Antonia brings in two cooked geese. After dinner, Rudolph, the oldest Cuzak boy, tells Jim the story about the Cutter murder. He tells Jim that Wick Cutter had bought a pistol and killed his wife and then shot himself, and he stayed alive long enough to boast to witnesses that he had outlived her. Rudolph asks Jim if he had ever known anyone who

had killed himself for spite. Jim takes a walk with Antonia and her husband in the orchard.

Anton tells Jim about his early life and that he came up from Florida after his orange crop failed. He tells Jim how he met and married Antonia. Jim observes that Anton Cuzak is a city man who is kept living in the country by Antonia's warm heart. He notices the love he has for his family.

Jim says good-bye to Antonia and her family as he takes the train back to Black Hawk in Chapter Three. He is bored and restless in town, and he is anxious for his train to arrive so that he may leave. While Jim is waiting for his train, he takes a long walk out of the town. He feels the beauty of the land and remembers his adventures with the Cuzak boys. He walks further on and notices the faint road that once led to his grandparent's farm. Jim remembers the first night he and Antonia arrived in the open wagon, and how their lives were shaped by the prairie.

Analysis

One of the great strengths of the novel lies in Willa Cather's use of parallels in this final book. The parallels Jim sees when he returns to see Antonia after twenty years serves to reawaken his love for the land, for Antonia, and for the memories of his boyhood. The first parallel comes with the news that Antonia has married a fellow Bohemian. This indicates that she has gone back to the roots of her old country and that she has remained true to her heritage. Her husband is a city person, and he leaves the city against his wishes to live a life in the country to appease Antonia. This parallels her own father's wish to stay in his own country, and how he gave that up. Mr. Shimerda appeased his wife by moving from Bohemia to America, just as Anton Cuzak appeases Antonia by moving from the city to the country. This parallel ends here, as Anton forges a positive attitude toward country life through the love of his family.

In another parallel, Jim finds out that Antonia is poor, just as she was when they first met as children. Jim is reluctant to visit her because of her poverty; he remembers Antonia's great struggle to survive with nothing and the tragic events that led to her father's suicide.

When he goes to visit the Cuzak farm, he is met by two of the younger Cuzak boys. They are mourning their dead dog by the side of the road, which indicates their love and respect for living things, and it serves as an indication that they have been brought up with a strong set of morals.

Jim finds the farm teeming with life: children are running around, and ducks, geese, and other assorted animals are walking about the yard. This sets the atmosphere here for Jim: he realizes this is a place full of life and happiness, an extension of the beauty of the land itself, where both man and nature co-exist in a peaceful and content dwelling.

Ms. Cather wants to emphasize the years that have come between Jim and Antonia. Jim sees relatively little change in her appearance. She is older and wiser, and she has maintained her robustness. Antonia does not recognize Jim at first, which tells us that she has forgotten him over the years. Though Jim never tells us of any physical change in himself, perhaps even the way he is dressed, we are led to believe he has changed. He has come back a successful lawyer, and he probably arrives well-dressed and affluent. This is apparent when Antonia explains to him that her husband is away, thinking Jim is a businessman.

After her recognition, Jim is introduced to Antonia's children. They come flocking to his side, and he is surprised to find they know so much about him. This evokes another realization for Jim: Antonia has not only kept alive their wonderful past in her own memory, she has passed it on to her children. This indicates that the stories will become immortal. They will be forever recycled.

The recycling process continues when Jim discovers that many of the Cuzak children can barely speak English. Again, this important detail ties the reader to the beginning of the novel when the Shimerdas first inhabit the prairie, speaking only their native language. Antonia has taught her children that language almost exclusively, solidifying her ties to both her heritage and her own past.

We see these ties strengthened further with Jim's visit to the fruit cave. Again the parallel manifests itself in the physical reality of the cave: Antonia's first house on the prairie was a cave dug into the side of the hill. In this fruit cave, the Cuzak's have stored barrels of fruit. The children show Jim pickles and watermelon rinds. The watermelon rinds, we remember, were something Antonia ate as a child with her Russian neighbors. The boys think that Jim has never seen spiced plums and ask their mother to show him. They refer to Jim as an "American," and they are surprised to find that Jim knows all about Antonia's recipes. It serves to illuminate in the children the long friendship between Jim and their mother.

Jim's walk through the orchard with Antonia rekindles his love for the land. He is amazed by the beauty that has shaped and evolved the countryside. He finds the same peace of mind that he found many years before while sitting alone in the pumpkin garden. Again, we see the children's respect for life and the land as they bury their dog in the orchard. We see a parallel to Jim's own love of trees in Antonia when she tells him she loves the trees in her orchard as if they were people. Jim visited the big elm tree on his pony rides as a boy, and remembered that it was like visiting a person.

Jim sees that the land and the life on the farm has shaped Antonia into the successful mother she has become. However, Antonia tells Jim that her town-life experiences really gave her the insight into raising children. Her years with the Harlings, and then with the Cutters, and her socializing at the dances, taught her many things, good and bad, about people. It taught her how to teach proper morals to her children.

When Antonia brings out the photographs, we see a blending of past, present, and future in one scene. When Antonia shows each photograph, the stories roll out from the memories of past moments as she tells a story of each character. The present manifests itself in the friendship that has been rekindled between Jim and Antonia. They both have aged well and mutually seek to maintain their friendship. The future projects itself through Antonia's children as they gather around to hear the stories from each of the photographs. The parallels that Ms. Cather weaves into this scene signifies a major theme of the novel, that of the endless cycle of things through time, through past, present, and future.

After the memories become awakened in Jim, he goes to the haymow to sleep with the boys. Here a curious contrast develops: the boys immediately go to sleep, while Jim lies awake and remembers his boyhood. This contrast serves to show us the power of reminiscence: the boys do not yet have the powerful memories from which they can tap into and so, they immediately fall asleep. Jim's lying awake serves as a metaphor for his own awakened memories, and that he is older and more shaped by life than the boys.

Jim has already developed a deep respect for Antonia's husband Anton before even meeting him. He has rescued her from her misfortune at the hands of Larry Donovan and made her a good wife and mother. Anton returns from the fair in a wagon with his eldest son. We see his kindness and generosity emerge when he brings out gifts from the fair and gives them to each of his children. Though he is poor and hard working, Anton establishes his affectionate character here, as he uses the little money he has and spends it on his children's happiness.

Woven throughout this novel is the act of storytelling. Stories are told in every section of the novel by an assortment of characters, and most notably by Antonia. Twenty years later, Jim finds this storytelling very much alive as Rudolph Cuzak tells the story of the Cutter murder. Because one of Antonia's children has been selected to tell the story, we see that the importance of storytelling will continue into the next generation. We are also tied in to events that occurred earlier in Cather's novel, giving it a sense of completion. Jim says his good-byes to Antonia and her family and goes back to Black Hawk to wait for his train home. His love for the country becomes solidified in this final chapter of the novel. He sees the town of Black Hawk as a boring and bland place. There is no one he knows in the town. Like the traveling salesmen at the hotel so many years before, Jim feels no sense of permanence in anything here. While waiting for his train, Jim takes a walk out of town. He remembers his most recent, pleasant memories with the Cuzak boys, and then he feels the beauty of the land he felt from his first moments here as a little boy. When he finds the faint trail that once led to his grandparent's farm, his memory reaches deep down to the very first night he arrived to his new home. From this vantage point, at the very beginning of his experience, Jim is able to see the great circle of life, the process of recycling. His own memory has come back to his ride through the darkness in the wagon the first night he arrived on the prairie, when he had no memory at all. This circle that he forms in his memory parallels the very circle of life implicit in the land itself, through the change of seasons, death, and rebirth.

Immortality, for Jim, comes in keeping alive the love of Antonia through the power of memory.

Study Questions

1. What did Jim send Antonia when he was in Prague?
2. From what does Antonia make kolaches?
3. Where does the narrator tell us that life "comes and goes" at a farmhouse?
4. Where does the children's teacher have the school picnic every year?
5. Who does Jim tell Antonia was once a great huntswoman but now shoots only clay pigeons?
6. What does Antonia do with her pictures of the old country?
7. What story does Charley Cuzak want Jim to tell?
8. How was Anton Cuzak dressed when Jim first met him?
9. What did the coroner find on Wick Cutter's desk?
10. Who was Anton Cuzak's cousin?

Answers

1. He sent her some photographs of her native village.
2. Antonia makes kolaches from spiced plums.
3. Life comes and goes by the back door.
4. She has the picnic in the Cuzak's grape arbour.
5. The Queen of Italy was once a great huntswoman.
6. She framed them and hung them in the parlour.
7. He wants to hear the story of Jim killing the rattlesnake.
8. He arrives in the heat in his Sunday clothes, a tailored jacket and a polka-dot bow tie.
9. He found a letter stating that he shot his wife, invalidating her will.
10. Anton Jelinek was Anton Cuzak's cousin.

Suggested Essay Topics

1. Explain Antonia's choice of names for each of her children and how each of these names ties in to characters from her past.
2. Discuss the differences between the Cuzak household and the Shimerda household from many years before.

SECTION SEVEN

Sample Analytical Paper Topics

The following paper topics are designed to test your understanding of the novel as a whole and to analyze important themes and literary devices. Following each topic is a sample outline to get you started.

Topic #1

When Mr. Shimerda dies, Antonia is left, through no choice of her own, without a father. She and her family are left poor and grieving in a strange new land. However, the rest of Antonia's life after his suicide becomes shaped by the choices that she makes. Explain how these choices cause change at various points of her life.

Outline

I. Thesis Statement: *After her father's death, all of the changes that occur in Antonia's life come from her own choices.*

II. Chooses to work like a man in the fields

  A. Develops knowledge of farming

  B. Foregoes her education with Jim

  C. Appreciates life on the land

III. Chooses to work for Harlings

  A. Becomes part of a warm and friendly family

  B. Learns to cook and sew

- C. Learns the mannerisms of town life
- D. Makes wages for spending

IV. Chooses to work for the Cutters
- A. Leaves happy family life of the Harlings
- B. Makes more money and does less work
- C. Becomes irresponsible with her free time
- D. Becomes victim to Wick Cutter's advances

V. Chooses to marry Larry Donovan
- A. Doesn't listen to others' opinions of him
- B. Leaves Black Hawk for Colorado
- C. Larry deserts her after a month
- D. Comes home and lives quietly on farm
- E. Bears her child alone

VI. Chooses to marry Anton Cuzak
- A. Meets and marries a fellow Bohemian
- B. Has many children
- C. Teaches them customs and language of the old country
- D. Lives a content and happy life on the prairie

VII. Conclusion: Despite some poor decisions, Antonia ends up happy and content with her life.

Topic #2

Many immigrants arrived on the Nebraska prairie from all over Europe. Most of them were very poor and they had little hope for survival. It can be said that the true meaning of their pioneer spirit rose from their perseverance, their sheer will to survive the harshest conditions. They braved the ordeals of prairie life for many years until they found comfort and established themselves in a new land. Discuss the many hardships these immigrants faced and how overcoming those hardships defined their pioneer spirit.

Outline

I. Thesis Statement: *Immigrants on the prairie encountered many hardships which they overcame through courage and hard work.*

II. Fighting the language barrier

  A. Cannot ask for help when they need it

  B. Shimerdas at the mercy of Krajiek

  C. Were forced to make friends with neighbors

III. Surviving the harshness of the prairie

  A. Mr. Shimerda has no knowledge of farming

  B. Poor living conditions

  C. Severe winters and snowstorms

IV. Dealing with psychological problems

  A. Mr. Shimerda's depression and suicide

  B. Mrs. Shimerda's bitterness

  C. Ambrosch's unfriendly demeanor

  D. Tragic story the wolves haunts Russian Peter

V. Prejudice from Americans

  A. Customs and food hard to tolerate

  B. Townspeople look down on them

VI. Conclusion: Despite all of their hardships, the immigrants that survived the harsh life of the prairie became true heroes and they will always be remembered.

Topic #3

Most of the characters in *My Antonia* are women. Willa Cather has chosen to represent many of these characters as successful and independent women, much like herself. Describe how the main female characters in this novel achieve and maintain their independence.

Outline

I. Thesis Statement: *Many of the females in* My Antonia *achieve a success and independence that had once been reserved for men.*

II. Antonia
   - A. Works farm like a man
   - B. Makes wages and spends money
   - C. Moves west
   - D. Becomes head of household on Cuzak farm

III. Frances Harling
   - A. Helps father in his business
   - B. Helps townspeople avoid Wick Cutter
   - C. Makes money and buys gifts

IV. Lena Lingard
   - A. Becomes dressmaker
   - B. Moves to Lincoln and opens shop
   - C. Won't marry and be subservient to a man
   - D. Lives a single, carefree life

V. Tiny Soderball
   - A. Works as a single woman at a hotel
   - B. Starts a lodging house in Seattle
   - C. Helps found Dawson City during gold rush
   - D. Moves to San Francisco a wealthy and independent woman

VI. Conclusion: Willa Cather is implying her own success as an independent woman by making many of her fictional female characters independent and successful.

Topic #4

Cather uses the seasons in this novel to symbolize life itself, using them to great effect in painting scenes. Each of these scenes show

how the endless cycle of spring-summer-fall-winter reflects and symbolizes the character's up-and-down struggles through life on the prairie. Describe the use of each season in the novel and what it symbolizes, using examples to support each symbol.

Outline

I. Thesis Statement: *Willa Cather uses the seasons to symbolize the recycling process of human emotions.*

II. Autumn means change and fulfillment

   A. Novel begins in autumn

   B. Harvest of crops brings contentment

   C. Sight of plough against sun means fulfillment

   D. Novel ends in autumn

III. Winter brings death and isolation

   A. Paralyzing snowstorms cause isolation from town

   B. Loneliness and then death of Mr. Shimerda

   C. Antonia delivers her baby alone

IV. Spring brings rebirth and hope

   A. Neighbors help build new Shimerda house

   B. Antonia moves away to get married

   C. Jim forges hopeful friendship with Lena

V. Summer is joy and life

   A. Dance tent comes to Black Hawk

   B. Jim begins new life at college

   C. Antonia lives happy life with Harlings

VI. Conclusion: By using the description of each season as a backdrop, we are able to connect each season to the highs and lows of the pioneer life.

Topic #5

Critics have noted that Willa Cather has set up a contrast in this novel: the European immigrants come across as idealistic and generous and full of personality, while the native settlers of Nebraska are dull and disliked. The immigrants who don't possess these admirable qualities never find success and happiness in the novel. Find examples of these differences in the characters of the novel.

Outline

I. Thesis Statement: *Willa Cather wants to emphasize the importance of character in surviving the ordeals of immigrant life on the prairie.*

II. Antonia is full of good qualities

  A. Praises Jim for killing snake

  B. Works hard in fields and at Harlings

  C. Learns English quickly from Jim

  D. Survives her fathers suicide and Larry Donovan's leaving her

III. Other hired girls have good qualities

  A. Lena wants to build a house for mother

  B. Lena runs her business with intelligence

  C. Lena has compassion for others and she cries in the theater

  D. Tiny is generous and independent

IV. Townspeople seem listless and unlikable

  A. Wick Cutter is devious and ugly

  B. Mrs. Cutter is loud and ugly

  C. Salesmen at the hotel are unlikable

  D. Townspeople at dances are dull and snobbish

V. Immigrants without admirable qualities don't become successful

  A. Russian Peter recounts his horrible deed and dies

B. Mr. Shimerda is feeble and weak-minded and dies

C. Mrs. Shimerda is miserable and lives unhappy life

D. Ambrosch is unfriendly and unlikable

VI. Conclusion: Through the fate or fortune of characters in the novel, Willa Cather depicts the importance of virtues by failure or success.

SECTION EIGHT

Bibliography

The following edition of the text was used for this study guide:

Cather, Willa. *My Antonia.* Boston: Houghton Mifflin Company, 1977.